Critical Guides to French Texts

95 Zola: Thérèse Raquin

Critical Guides to French Texts

EDITED BY ROGER LITTLE, WOLFGANG VAN EMDEN, DAVID WILLIAMS

ZOLA

Thérèse Raquin

Russell Cousins

Senior Lecturer in French
University of Birmingham

Grant & Cutler Ltd
1992

ISBN 0 7293 0345 4

I.S.B.N. 84-599-3299-0

DEPÓSITO LEGAL: V. 3.590-1992

Printed in Spain by
Artes Gráficas Soler, S.A., Valencia
for
GRANT & CUTLER LTD
55-57 GREAT MARLBOROUGH STREET, LONDON W1V 2AY

Contents

Preface   7

1. Background   9

2. Realist Intentions   15

3. People   29

4. Narrative Structure   40

5. The Horror Story   51

6. Theatre   62

7. Cinema   72

Select Bibliography   85

For Matthew, Felicity and Sophie

Preface

The protestations of outrage which greeted the publication of *Thérèse Raquin* in 1867 have long since joined the many faded curiosities of literary history. That Zola should have been accused of writing a lurid, pornographic work will doubtless appear risible to the modern reader; that the author should have claimed in self-defence to have written a *scientific* novel may seem even more ludicrous.

The present study attempts to bring these positions into sharper focus by examining Zola's aims in the context of the evolving realist mode in nineteenth-century French fiction. After an account of the novel's genesis and publication, the author's theory and practice are tested in terms of his realist intentions, the presentation of his protagonists, the construction of the narrative, and his fiction's affinities with the Gothic novel. The final two chapters examine the successive evolutions of Zola's tale, from his own stage adaptation to those by other dramatists, and from the early silent screen versions to Marcel Carné's modernized reworking for the cinema.

Thérèse Raquin marks a significant stage in Zola's development as a writer. It is the first of his early novels to break with the confessional style, and where, by distancing himself from the characters and situations, he achieves a disciplined and tightly-organized narrative. At the same time, with its depiction of individuals as an expression of a given heredity and of environmental forces, the novel anticipates the monumental twenty-volume family saga, *Les Rougon-Macquart* (1871-93). Of the individual novels in this series, *La Bête humaine* (1890), in which Zola returns to the themes of sexual passion, adultery and murder, has a particular affinity with *Thérèse Raquin*.

My discussion owes much to the scholarship of others, not least of all to the work of John Lapp and Henri Mitterand, to whom all students of *Thérèse Raquin* have long been indebted, but also to the more recent contributions of Robert Lethbridge. To these, and to the other Zolists I have drawn on, may I acknowledge my debt and express my gratitude.

Page references in the text are to the Folio edition of Zola's novel which was first published in 1979. Articles and books cited in the course of discussion are listed in the Bibliography and indicated in the text by an italicized reference number.

1. Background

'Imaginez que Furbice ait épousé
Margaï (...)'. (Zola, Introduction to
Un Mariage d'amour, *Le Figaro*,
24 December 1866)

Sources

The origins of *Thérèse Raquin* are both simple and complex. Zola
identifies the immediate source as his own short story, *Un Mariage
d'amour*, published on 24 December 1866 in *Le Figaro*. However,
this story was itself prompted by the newspaper's serialization of *La
Vénus de Gordes*, a colourful tale of adultery and murder, by
Adolphe Belot and Ernest Daudet. In his introduction to *Un Mariage
d'amour*, Zola acknowledges this serial as his stimulus, and signals
his intention to rework his story as a novel: 'Le roman que publie *Le
Figaro* et qui obtient un si légitime succès d'émotion me rappelle une
terrible histoire de passion et de souffrance. Je vais la conter en
quelques mots, me réservant d'écrire un jour le volume qu'elle
demanderait' (p.338, note 21).

La *Vénus de Gordes*, derived from a famous criminal trial, is a
diffuse and exotic tale. The heroine Margaï, 'la Vénus de Gordes',
deceives her husband Pascoul with Furbice, a local horse-dealer.
Fearing discovery, the adulterous couple shoot Pascoul and unsuc-
cessfully accuse a faithful servant, Moulinet, of their crime. The
couple are given life-sentences and exiled to Cayenne Island, but
Furbice escapes en route. The devoted Moulinet follows Margaï to
Cayenne, and marries her. However, she succumbs to yellow fever,
and the distraught Moulinet drowns himself in the sea with her body.

Although Zola's *Un Mariage d'amour* shares the initial
premise of adultery leading to murder, it assumes a new direction by

exploring the hypothesis that the murderers escape detection and get married: 'Imaginez que Furbice ait épousé Margaï (...). Les deux meurtriers, l'amant et la femme adultère, ont sauvé leur honneur; ils vont maintenant vivre la vie de félicité qu'ils ont rêvée; les voilà réunis à jamais, liés par la volupté et par le sang, pouvant contenter enfin à l'aise leurs appétits de richesse et de luxure.' Their anticipated bliss, however, is frustrated by an overwhelming sense of guilt, and it is this burden therefore, and not the judgement of the courts, which becomes their punishment: 'le coupable trouvant une effroyable punition dans l'impunité même de son crime' (p.338, note 21).

In contrast to the colourful locations of *La Vénus de Gordes*, Zola's story has a more mundane Parisian setting, and a cast of three: Suzanne and Michel, the married couple, and Jacques, the husband's friend and wife's lover. The adulterous couple drown Michel in the Seine, but during a struggle he bites Jacques's cheek, leaving a permanent scar. The couple successfully pass off the murder as a boating accident. A visit to the Morgue to identify the corpse brings unbearable nightmares. The murderers marry, but the imagined presence of the drowned Michel destroys their pleasure. The anguished couple, acknowledging their crime, commit suicide.

The links between *Un Mariage d'amour* and the future *Thérèse Raquin* are clear. The novel's plot exists here in embryo, though without the important accretions of Mme Raquin and the secondary participants, namely Grivet, Michaud, Olivier, Suzanne and the cat, François. Little remains of *La Vénus de Gordes*.

As Henri Mitterand (*32*) has shown, additional sources for Zola's novel may be traced to two earlier works: *L'Assassinat du Pont-Rouge* (1859) by Charles Barbara, and *Atar-Gull* (1831) by Eugène Sue. To the former, Zola may have been indebted for the character Michaud, Camille's ghostly presence, and Thérèse's fear that a child by Laurent would resemble her dead husband. To the latter, Zola may owe the conception of Mme Raquin as the paralysed mother attempting to denounce her son's killers.

Composition and serialization

The first firm evidence of Zola's commitment to a novel based on his short story is found in a letter dated 12 February 1867 to Arsène Houssaye, director of *La Revue du XIXe siècle*: 'J'ai songé à la nouvelle que je pourrais bien écrire pour la *Revue*, et voilà que cette nouvelle est devenue un roman dans ma tête.(...) Je prendrai pour sujet l'histoire que j'ai contée brièvement un jour dans *Le Figaro*: *Un Mariage d'amour*' (*20*, 1, pp.470-71). A serialization in three instalments was agreed, and on 4 March 1867 Zola despatched the first chapters for publication in May, with the remainder promised for the June and July issues (*20*, 1, p.478). At the end of May, Zola informed his friend Antony Valabrègue that the novel was almost finished: 'Je suis très content du roman psychologique et physiologique que je vais publier dans la *Revue du XIXe siècle*. Ce roman, qui est écrit presque entièrement, sera à coup sûr ma meilleure oeuvre' (*20*, 1, p.500). However, Zola's ambitions suffered a temporary setback when in June, a month before the already-delayed serialization was due to begin, the review folded. After fresh negotiations the novel eventually appeared in another periodical, *L'Artiste*, between August and October 1867. Meanwhile, Albert Lacroix had agreed to publish *Thérèse Raquin* in November.

Publication

More than once, Zola considered changing the title of his novel. In a letter dated 9 June 1867, he wrote: 'J'attends les épreuves d'*Un Mariage d'amour*, dont je changerai sans doute le titre' (*20*, 1, p.511). He again aired this possibility in a letter to Lacroix, dated 13 September 1867: 'Quant au titre, il sera d'autant meilleur, selon moi, qu'il sera plus simple. L'oeuvre s'intitule dans *L'Artiste*: *Un Mariage d'amour*, mais je compte changer cela et mettre: *Thérèse Raquin*, le nom de l'héroïne' (*20*, 1, p.523). Zola also suggested the subtitle *étude* to indicate his analytical approach, but Lacroix was not persuaded, and when the first edition was officially registered on

7 December 1867, the covers carried the simple title: *Thérèse Raquin*.

Nevertheless, Zola had signalled his approach in his choice of epigraph for the novel: 'Le vice et la vertu sont des produits comme le vitriol et le sucre'. Taken from the *Introduction à la littérature anglaise* (1863) by the respected positivist philosopher and critic Hippolyte Taine, the quotation was intended to legitimate the objective, morally-detached stance favoured by contemporary realists. Within four months the initial printing had sold out, and when the second edition reached the bookshops in April 1868, readers found that Zola had replaced this quotation with a preface, in which he sought to answer hostile criticism and to clarify his intentions.

Critical reception

Critics were horrified by Zola's professed clinical study which they condemned as naïve in concept, crude in execution and questionable in moral stance. A. Desonnaz (*25*) presented the novel as a debased, tasteless exercise in sensationalism by a writer devoid of literary talent: '*Thérèse Raquin* est une oeuvre tourmentée, d'une conception vulgaire et d'une exécution secondaire (...). A défaut d'un sentiment élevé de l'art, on a recours à des émotions de cours d'assises ou à des dissections d'amphithéâtre.' The critic H. Pellerin (*34*) judged the novel to be excessive in its descriptions, and morally suspect: 'Jamais on n'a tracé avec des couleurs plus crues l'image des passions poussées jusqu'à la rage. C'est d'un réalisme épouvantable.(...) je suis d'avis que l'esprit serait mieux employé à faire autre chose que des livres dont l'utilité, au point de vue moral, est très contestable.' For Firmin Boissin (*22*), Zola had misused his undoubted talents: 'Jamais le réalisme ne s'était affiché avec tant de brutalité et, il faut bien le dire aussi, avec tant de puissance. Beaucoup de talent au service d'une littérature des plus immorales et des plus malsaines. Toute une vie passée dans la boue, le sang et l'amour bestial, se terminant par un double suicide: tel est le bilan de *Thérèse Raquin*. Je ne puis en dire davantage.' The most ostensibly ferocious attack on the novel, and on the realist movement in general, came from the critic Louis

Ulbach[1] who, writing under his pseudonym Ferragus in *Le Figaro* dated 23 January 1868, headed his piece 'La Littérature putride'. He accused realist authors of cheapening literature by a sordid sensationalism and a pornographic preoccupation with physiological details. Such authors are dismissed as 'une école monstrueuse (...) qui fait appel aux curiosités les plus chirurgicales' (p.319). Their shocking explicitness had detracted from their declared moral and social purpose. A reworking of criminal cases was no substitute for creative talent, and the severe limitations of their methods were evident in their insubstantial characters, 'tous ces fantômes impossibles' (p.320), who would never translate successfully to the stage.

After this preamble, Zola's novel is roundly condemned as 'une flaque de boue', and is seen to encapsulate the worst features of the realist mode: 'Quant à *Thérèse Raquin*, c'est le résidu de toutes les horreurs publiées précédemment. On y a égoutté tout le sang et toutes les infamies' (p.322). The author's approach is likened to that of the reviled Impressionists: 'il [Zola] voit la femme comme M. Manet la peint, couleur de boue avec des maquillages roses' (p.321). The excesses of the realist writers had to be checked: 'Ce livre résume trop fidèlement toutes les putridités de la littérature contemporaine pour ne pas soulever un peu de colère. (...) Forçons les romanciers à prouver leur talent autrement que par des emprunts aux tribunaux et à la voirie' (p.323).

In a dismissive rejoinder published in *Le Figaro* dated 31 January 1867, Zola concerned himself principally with two points. He ridiculed the concept that a novel's characters should be judged according to their plausibility as theatrical creations, 'cette incroyable façon de juger deux genres de littérature si différents' (p.325), and asserted that realist fiction, in its frank portrayal of human vice, did serve a valuable moralising function: 'La vérité, comme le feu, purifie tout' (p.327).

However, Zola's detractors were rarely convinced by such arguments, and some form of censorship was to be expected. In his

---

[1] Armand Lanoux suggests that Ulbach and Zola, two seasoned journalists, colluded in their controversy to promote the novel. See: *Bonjour, Monsieur Zola*, Paris, Hachette, 1962, p.97.

letter to Valabrègue of 29 May 1867, Zola wrote of his novel: 'Je crois m'y être mis coeur et chair. Je crains même de m'y être mis un peu trop en chair et d'émouvoir Monsieur le procureur impérial. Il est vrai que quelques mois de prison ne me font pas peur' (*20*, 1, p.500). Although the Public Prosecutor raised no objections to *Thérèse Raquin*, the commission regulating the sale of books by hawkers did impose a ban. Zola responded with an open letter in *La Tribune* dated 9 August 1868. Once more he firmly reiterated his claim to the scientific value of his work: '*Thérèse Raquin* est une étude de savant, l'anatomie exacte d'une maladie humaine particulière' (*21*, 10, p.757).

Throughout, Zola had steadfastly defended *Thérèse Raquin* as a work belonging to a realist tradition, and inspired by contemporary scientific views and methodology. A closer examination of that defence within the realist context, together with Zola's practice in the novel itself, is now required.

2. Realist Intentions

'Le vent est à la science; nous sommes poussés malgré nous vers l'étude exacte des faits et des choses'
(Zola, *Les Réalistes du Salon*, 1866)

In the course of the 1860s Zola's views on art and literature had evolved from an initial commitment to the aesthetics of realism to a self-proclaimed naturalism. The terms realism and naturalism require clarification.

Zola's discovery of Balzac, Stendhal, Flaubert and Champfleury was decisive in shaping his conception of literary realism. From the practice and precepts of these writers it was understood that the overtly personal and confessional, the sentimental and sensational, the idealized and the didactic were to be shunned in favour of a more self-disciplined, more factual, more objective account of the human condition. Realist writers were perceived as conscientious observers of the shaping forces in contemporary society, and of the consequences those forces held for ordinary men and women. Idealized heroes and heroines, engaged in dramatic undertakings, were replaced by more matter-of-fact, common people caught up in everyday situations and coping as best they might. Rigorous documentation and the application of scientific methodology were held to be of greater consequence than inventiveness or literary technique. A complete and accurate depiction of an individual's material conditions was the prerequisite to understanding behaviour, and since the ensuing explanation was deemed to be purely factual and objective, moral reflection was considered an inappropriate intrusion.

The application of the scientific, analytical approach to literature had been encouraged by the influential critic Hippolyte Taine.

In the preface to his *Histoire de la littérature anglaise* (1863), he argued that in order to appreciate a national culture or the work of an individual artist it was imperative to examine the major formative influences, namely 'la race, le milieu, le moment'. The critic's task, moreover, was to provide an understanding of the writer's works which was free from moral preconceptions. Zola's enthusiastic endorsement of this approach is apparent both from his quotation from Taine used to head the first edition of *Thérèse Raquin*, and also from his article published in *Mes Haines* (1866), recording the critic's achievements: 'La nouvelle science, faite de physiologie et de psychologie, d'histoire et de philosophie, a eu son épanouissement en lui [Taine]. Il est, dans notre époque, la manifestation la plus haute de nos curiosités, de nos besoins d'analyse, de nos désirs de réduire toutes choses au pur mécanisme des sciences mathématiques' (*21*, 10, p.155).

Taine's position was complemented by the work of the positivist philosopher Emile Deschanel whose book, *La Physiologie des écrivains* (1864), borrowed from contemporary medical theories to focus attention on the role of temperament in creativity. For Zola, this method would be applied to fictional characters.

A growing awareness of scientific methodology, and a greater familiarity with medical literature, led the emerging generation of realist writers to place even greater emphasis on biological and environmental factors in their representation of human behaviour. The method was already implicit in the work of Flaubert, and this aspect of *Madame Bovary* had already excited the attention of the critic Sainte-Beuve, whose observation 'Anatomistes et physiologistes, je vous retrouve partout' in *Le Moniteur universel* of 4 May 1857, had perceptively anticipated the future trend.

Schooled in the basic tenets of the realist mode, novelists stressed the importance of documentary investigation, and, insisting on the scientific value of their studies, they readily styled themselves 'anatomists' and 'physiologists'. The terminology of medical science became part of their vocabulary, so that words like *anatomie*, *physiologie*, *analyse*, *névrose*, *dissection* and *éréthisme*, became the common currency of works of fiction as well as of learned papers.

As social observers guided by scientific principles of accuracy and objectivity, realist authors aimed to communicate the results of their literary experiments candidly and without moral assumption. Naturalism, with its commitment to documentation and an analytical approach, shares common ground with realist practice, but, in its additional emphasis on biological theory informing that analysis, it is more deterministic in its presentation of the human animal. Guided by their new knowledge, naturalist writers would demonstrate that patterns of behaviour were both determined and predictable. Zola, in his preface to *Thérèse Raquin*, associates himself with the aims and methods of 'le groupe d'écrivains naturalistes' (p.29), and from his correspondence and literary criticism of this period, it is possible to trace the development of this commitment to naturalist concepts.

In a letter to Antony Valabrègue dated 18 August 1864, Zola had defined his understanding of realism as one of three literary conventions. These are presented in historical terms as the Classical, the Romantic, and the Realist. Each convention is likened to a screen of a different transparency through which the writer relates to objective reality. Zola's preference was for the realist screen which aimed at the minimum of distortion: 'L'Ecran réaliste est un simple verre à vitre, très mince, très clair, et qui a la prétention d'être si parfaitement transparent que les images le traversent et se reproduisent ensuite dans toute leur réalité' (*20*, 1, p.379).

In October 1864, the Goncourt brothers published *Germinie Lacerteux*, a fictionalized account of their servant's decline into alcoholism and debauchery. The authors defended their uncompromising study by invoking the criteria of medical science: 'aujourd'hui que le roman s'est imposé les études et les devoirs de la science, il peut en revendiquer les libertés et les franchises' (*16*, p.2). Their novel was nothing less than a conscientious case-study: 'l'étude qui suit est la clinique de l'Amour' (ibid., p.1).

Zola's review of the novel in *Le Salut public* of 24 February 1865 was enthusiastic. He praised the authors for their informed clinical approach, 'la grande place qu'ils ont accordée à l'observation physiologique' (*21*, 10, p.70), and endorsed their claim to freedom of inquiry: 'l'artiste a le droit de fouiller en pleine nature humaine, de ne rien voiler du cadavre humain' (ibid., p.69).

The notion of the writer as observer and analyst is again central to Zola's deliberations on the novel which were presented to the Congrès scientifique de France held at Aix-en-Provence in December 1866. In his paper *Deux définitions du roman*, he traced the evolution of the genre to contemporary realist practice: 'nous en sommes aujourd'hui au roman analytique qui a pour but de peindre la nature telle qu'elle est et les hommes tels qu'ils sont' (*21*, 10, p.281). The distinguishing characteristics of modern fiction are seen as observation and analysis, and, with Balzac clearly in mind, Zola defines the 'romancier analyste' as follows:

> Il est, avant tout, un savant, un savant de l'ordre moral. J'aime à me le représenter comme l'anatomiste de l'âme et de la chair. Il dissèque l'homme, étudie le jeu des passions, interroge chaque fibre, fait l'analyse de l'organisme entier. Comme le chirurgien, il n'a ni honte ni répugnance, lorsqu'il fouille les plaies humaines. Il n'a souci que de vérité, et étale devant nous le cadavre de notre coeur. Les sciences modernes lui ont donné pour instrument l'analyse et la méthode expérimentale. Il procède comme nos chimistes et nos mathématiciens; il décompose les actions, en détermine les causes, en explique les résultats; il opère selon des équations fixes, ramenant les faits à l'étude de l'influence des milieux sur les individualités. Le nom qui lui convient est celui de docteur ès sciences morales. (*21*, 10, p.281)

However, Zola's conception of the novel as a dispassionate scientific examination of human behaviour did not meet with universal acceptance. The application of his theories in *Thérèse Raquin* provoked a storm of critical protest, and in his preface to the novel's second edition he sought to dispel a number of misunderstandings and misrepresentations.

Zola reformulated many of the arguments previously advanced in his defence of realist fiction to refute the charge of pornography. He reaffirmed the serious scientific nature of his work; 'mon but a été un but scientifique avant tout' (p.24), and drew a parallel with clinical investigations: 'Qu'on lise le roman avec soin, on verra que chaque chapitre est l'étude d'un cas curieux de physiologie' (p.25). He had proceeded as though he were a doctor conducting an autopsy: 'J'ai simplement fait sur deux corps vivants le travail analytique que les chirurgiens font sur des cadavres' (p.25). He had, accordingly, reported his findings in the same dispassionate manner as the scientist, or indeed with the same detachment as the painter working with a nude model: 'L'humanité des modèles disparaissait comme elle disparaît aux yeux de l'artiste qui a une femme nue vautrée devant lui, et qui songe uniquement à mettre cette femme sur sa toile dans la vérité de ses formes et de ses colorations' (p.25). Accusations of pornographic intent were firmly rebutted: ' Tant que j'ai écrit *Thérèse Raquin*, j'ai oublié le monde, je me suis perdu dans la copie exacte et minutieuse de la vie, me donnant tout entier à l'analyse du mécanisme humain, et je vous assure que les amours cruelles de Thérèse et Laurent n'avaient pour moi rien d'immoral, rien qui puisse pousser aux passions mauvaises' (p.25).

Zola's repeated claims to an objective presentation do not, however, stand up to close scrutiny. His descriptions, in practice, are often highly evocative, and have been more regularly compared to Impressionist canvasses than to the measured prose of a coroner's report. The comparison is apposite, for there is little doubt that Zola's association with the emerging group of artists was of considerable importance to the development of his own descriptive techniques in *Thérèse Raquin*.

The author's formative association with Cézanne and Manet, his appreciation of their aims, and the parallels with his own work, have been carefully documented and analysed.[2] The author not only

---

[2]See: F.W.J. Hemmings, 'Zola, Manet and the Impressionists', *PMLA*, no. 73 (1968), pp.407-17; Joy Newton, 'Emile Zola Impressionniste', *Les Cahiers naturalistes*, Vol. XIII, nos 33-34 (1967) pp.39-52, 124-38; Rodolphe

promoted the Impressionists through his journalism, but also attempted to reproduce their effects in his fiction. According to H. Hertz, Zola defined his relationship with the painters as follows: 'Je les ai traduits en littérature, par les touches, notes, colorations, par la palette de beaucoup de mes descriptions.(...) Les peintres m'ont aidé à peindre d'une manière neuve, "littérairement"' (*29*, p.32). In the specific case of *Thérèse Raquin*, Robert Lethbridge (*31*) has demonstrated the close affinities between Manet's *Olympia* and the portraiture of Thérèse, while Zola's description of the outing to Saint-Ouen has invited reference to other contemporary canvasses, such as Manet's *Le Déjeuner sur l'herbe*, Renoir's *Le Moulin à la Galette*, and Courbet's *Les Demoiselles des bords de la Seine*.

Three key sections of the narrative, the description of the Passage du Pont-Neuf, the episode of Camille's murder, and the scene at the Morgue serve to illustrate the divide between Zola's stated intention and his creative practice.

(i) The Passage du Pont-Neuf

In the novel's opening pages Zola introduces the Passage du Pont-Neuf. The techniques of documentary realism are evident in his carefully drawn picture, first of the arcade, then of the shop itself. Reference to the adjoining thoroughfares locates the precise area of Paris: 'Au bout de la rue Guénégaud (...) on trouve le passage du Pont-Neuf (...) qui va de la rue Mazarine à la rue de Seine' (p.31). The arcade's dimensions are noted in guide-book fashion: 'Ce passage a trente pas de long et deux de large, au plus' (p.31). Methodically, Zola sets the scene: 'A gauche, se creusent des boutiques (...). A droite, sur toute la longueur du passage, s'étend une muraille (...). Au-dessus du vitrage, la muraille monte (...)' (pp.31-32). The omniscient guide charts the arcade's changing appearance throughout the year and throughout the day: 'Par les beaux jours d'été (...). Par les vilains jours d'hiver (...). Toute la journée (...). Le soir (...)' (pp.31-32). The present tense lends the description an air of actuality and authenticity, while the impersonal 'on' suggests a detached observer: 'lorsqu'on vient des quais, on trouve (...)' (p.31); 'On y voit des apprentis (...) on y voit encore des vieillards' (p.32).

Once the arcade has been established, the descriptive present tense gives way to a narrative imperfect, and the focus narrows to the Raquin shop: 'Il y a quelques années (...) se trouvait une boutique' (p.33). Zola's exposition is again systematic. After details of the exterior, attention is directed to the window displays: 'A droite et à gauche s'enfonçaient des vitrines profondes (...). D'un côté, il y avait un peu de lingerie (...). De l'autre côté (...) s'étageaient de gros pelotons de laine' (pp.33-34). An inventory of the shop's interior is completed with a tour of the first-floor living accommodation. The objectivity of the description is guaranteed through the device of anonymous observers: 'les passants peuvent alors distinguer' (p.33); or the use of the unidentified 'on', as in 'on distinguait' (p.34) and 'on ne voyait pas' (p.34); or finally, through the equally impersonal formulation 'le regard ne pouvait distinguer' (p.33).

Although the exposition is methodical and detailed, a detached presentation is not sustained. The neutral tone gives way to subjectivity, with qualifications such as 'ignoble' (p.31), 'horrible' (p.32), 'misérablement' (p.31), 'lamentablement' (p.34) and the speculative 'sans doute' (p.34), while a personal reaction is explicit in Zola's description of the room: 'La pièce paraissait nue, glaciale' (p.35). The author's rhetorical presence is again apparent in comparisons and associations: 'la muraille (...) comme couverte d'une lèpre et toute couturée de cicatrices' (p.32); or 'Le passage prend l'aspect sinistre d'un véritable coupe-gorge' (p.33); or 'on dirait une galerie souterraine vaguement éclairée par trois lampes funéraires' (p.33). Each comparison promotes a particular perception of a given reality, rather than the reality itself. The suggestions of violence and death appropriately foreshadow the drama to unfold, but their inclusion is strictly at variance with the aims of the objective reporter concerned solely with a factual account.

The distinctly uninviting atmosphere of the arcade is promoted through a series of negations and a repeated emphasis on its dark, dank features. Human contact is rare in the arcade: 'Le passage du

Pont-Neuf n'est pas un lieu de promenade. On le prend pour éviter
un détour (...) personne ne parle, personne ne stationne' (p.32). The
dozing shop-keeper (p.33); the unsold stock, 'des marchandises
oubliées là depuis vingt ans' (p.32); the goods left fading in the
windows, 'un entassement d'objets ternes et fanés qui dormaient'
(p.34); all suggest a lack of commercial activity. A chilling
dampness permeates the whole area. The arcade, with its 'dalles
gluantes' (p.31), and 'suant toujours une humidité âcre' (p.31), is
swept by 'des souffles froids de caveau' (p.31), and 'des souffles
humides' (p.33). The shop itself exudes dampness, 'les boiseries (...)
suaient l'humidité par toutes leurs fentes' (p.33), and the interior is
'glaciale' (p.35). The depressing gloom which characterizes the
locality is conveyed by successive allusions to darkness. The words
noir, *sombre*, *obscure*, *ombre*, *lugubre*, *ténèbres*, *crépuscule* and *nuit*
colour the text, and the effect is reinforced by personification, as in
'où la nuit habite pendant le jour' (p.33), or 'des ténèbres qui
régnaient dans la boutique' (p.34). For Thérèse, the dank shop
conjures up a tomb: 'il lui sembla qu'elle descendait dans la terre
grasse d'une fosse' (p.47), and the murky interior dissolves into an
expressionistic abstraction as 'une ombre humide' (p.51). Cold, dark,
and damp, the shop carries intimations of death, anticipating both
Camille's watery grave and the chilling atmosphere of the Morgue.

Although Zola appeals to a range of senses in his evocation of
the Passage du Pont-Neuf, particular emphasis is placed on the
visual. In painting his gloomy canvas, Zola reveals an understanding
of the relationship between colour and the ambient light quality. The
absence of clear light is translated by the muddy hues of *jaunâtre*,
noirâtre, *verdâtre*, *bleuâtre* and *blanchâtre*. Diffused or refracted
light endows the shop with a disturbing eeriness: 'les vitrines, faites
de petits carreaux, moirent étrangement les marchandises de reflets
verdâtres; au-delà, derrière les étalages, les boutiques pleines de
ténèbres sont autant de trous lugubres dans lesquels s'agitent des
formes bizarres' (pp.31-32). Similarly, the appearance of items
displayed in the windows is conditioned by the dimly-filtered
daylight:

> La vitrine, de haut en bas, se trouvait ainsi emplie de loques blanchâtres qui prenaient un aspect lugubre dans l'obscurité transparente. Les bonnets neufs, d'un blanc plus éclatant, faisaient des taches crues sur le papier bleu dont les planches étaient garnies. Et, accrochées le long d'une tringle, les chaussettes de couleur mettaient des notes sombres dans l'effacement blafard et vague de la mousseline. (p.34)

The description reveals that Zola has more interest in rendering the quality of the light and the resulting appearance of the goods than in the goods themselves. His description recalls the linguistic impressionism of the Goncourt brothers. There is the use of the abstract quality-noun, as in 'l'effacement blafard et vague de la mousseline' which shifts attention from the object to the quality associated with the object; there is the preference for nominal syntax, as in 'faisaient des taches crues' or 'mettaient des notes sombres' where commonplace verbs yield emphasis to the noun, and the use of the substantivized colour-adjective 'd'un blanc plus éclatant' which again draws attention to the quality of the colour itself.

Zola's contention that he had simply engaged in a neutral transcription of observed reality is less than convincing. In his evocation of the atmosphere of Le Passage du Pont-Neuf, with its sinister overtones of violence, death and entombment, the author has not merely provided a verbal picture of his chosen location, he has created a tonal structure for the ensuing drama.

In a letter dated 10 June 1868, the critic Sainte-Beuve challenged Zola's depiction of the arcade: 'Je connais ce passage autant que personne (...). Eh bien! ce n'est pas vrai, c'est fantastique de description (...). Le passage est plat, banal, laid, surtout étroit, mais il n'a pas toute cette noirceur profonde et ces teintes à la Rembrandt que vous lui prêtez. C'est là une manière aussi d'être infidèle' (*21*, 1, p.680). A decade later, in an appreciation of Sainte-Beuve published in *Le Messager d'Europe* of October 1879, Zola conceded that completely objective descriptions were impossible: 'il

faut admettre que les lieux ont simplement la tristesse ou la gaieté
que nous y mettons' (*21*, 12, p.443).

(ii) The murder of Camille

The account of Camille's drowning provides a further test for Zola's
method of presentation. A dispassionate coroner's report, objectively
charting the circumstances of the victim's death, is not to be found.
Zola's practice is to intervene and to dramatize.

The narrator's voice is frequently heard foregrounding character, interpreting action, or commenting on events. Emotive terms
govern the description of Camille, who is variously qualified as 'ce
pauvre homme' (p.110) or 'le malheureux' (p.112), while for the
mediating Laurent he is 'exaspérant et ignoble' (p.105). Zola
intervenes to reveal Camille's feelings about the boat trip: 'La vérité
était que le commis avait une peur horrible de l'eau' (p.109). He
comments on the death-struggle as 'le spectacle horrible de la lutte'
(p.112), and pointedly reflects on the outcome: 'La nature aidait à la
sinistre comédie qui venait de se jouer' (p.113).

A tense mood is created for the murder episode. Laurent's
evident frustration and barely-controlled violent instincts charge the
scene by the river with menace. Tension rises with the information
that Laurent has devised a plan for 'un meurtre commode et sans
danger pour lui' (p.106), and intensifies when, in a whisper, he alerts
Thérèse to his intentions: '"Prends garde (...) je vais le jeter à l'eau"'
(p.109). The peaceful, natural setting becomes an ironic backcloth to
the impending human violence, while a cruel dramatic irony is
contained in Camille's observation on the coldness of the river: '"Il
ne ferait pas bon de piquer une tête dans ce bouillon-là"' (p.111).

With the darkening evening comes a chill, funereal gloom: 'Le
crépuscule venait. De grandes ombres tombaient des arbres, et les
eaux étaient noires sur les bords (...); les chants, les cris arrivaient,
vagues et mélancoliques, avec des langueurs tristes (...). Des
fraîcheurs traînaient. Il faisait froid' (p.110). The suggestions of
death are highlighted by Zola's intercalated reflections:

> Rien n'est plus douloureusement calme qu'un crépuscule
> d'automne. Les rayons pâlissent dans l'air frissonnant, les
> arbres vieillis jettent leurs feuilles. La campagne, brûlée
> par les rayons ardents de l'été, sent la mort venir avec les
> premiers vents froids. Et il y a, dans les cieux, des
> souffles plaintifs de désespérance. La nuit descend de
> haut, apportant des linceuls dans son ombre. (p.110)

The attribution of human emotions to the natural world places the
description squarely in the tradition of pathetic fallacy as, once more,
creation of mood assumes primacy over observed reality.

Throughout this episode the techniques of linguistic impressionism are again apparent. Zola's atmospheric evocations of the
setting give prominence to light-values, as in his rendering of the
sun-drenched dusty road, where he uses a plural abstract quality-
noun to draw attention to the reflected glare: 'La route, couverte de
poussière, largement éclairée par le soleil, avait des blancheurs
aveuglantes de neige' (p.110). Finally, in the dwindling light, the
landscape is transformed into patches of colour: 'Les grandes masses
rougeâtres devenaient sombres; tout le paysage se simplifiait dans le
crépuscule; la Seine, le ciel, les îles, les coteaux n'étaient plus que
des taches brunes et grises qui s'effaçaient au milieu d'un brouillard
laiteux' (p.111).

(iii) The Morgue

The identification of Camille's body at the Morgue offers the most
apt opportunity for a clinically-detached description, but, in a carefully stage-managed presentation, Zola exploits characterial
responses to create disturbing effects.

The Morgue is introduced as a theatre of horrors:

> La Morgue est un spectacle à la portée de toutes les
> bourses (...). Il y a des amateurs qui font un détour pour
> ne pas manquer une de ces représentations de la mort
> (...). Lorsque les dalles sont bien garnies (...) les visiteurs

se pressent, se donnent des émotions à bon marché,
s'épouvantent, plaisantent, applaudissent ou sifflent,
comme au théâtre... (p.127)

Zola's presentation is itself theatrical. In this 'spectacle' (pp.126,
128), he takes the reader through a series of gruesome tableaux
leading up to the horrendous climax when Laurent recognizes his
victim's putrescent corpse: 'Il n'avait pas encore vu un noyé si
épouvantable' (p.129).

Zola exploits Laurent's sensibilities to stress the human
response to the horrors of death. Camille's murderer is overwhelmed
by the smell of sanitized flesh: 'une odeur fade, une odeur de chair
lavée l'écoeurait' (p.124). A cold dampness penetrates his clothing:
'des souffles froids couraient sur sa peau; l'humidité des murs
semblait alourdir ses vêtements' (p.124). The damp stench becomes
almost unbearable: 'sa chair se révoltait, le dégoût et l'effroi
s'emparaient de son être, dès qu'il se trouvait dans l'humidité et
l'odeur fade de la salle' (p.126).

The visit turns into a nightmare: 'Il ne savait plus, il restait
frissonnant en face de ces haillons verdâtres qui semblaient se
moquer avec des grimaces horribles' (p.125). He is gripped by the
grotesque appearances of the bodies: 'd'autres semblaient des tas de
viandes sanglantes et pourries' (p.125), or: 'Le corps semblait un tas
de chairs dissoutes' (p.129). The decaying corpses shock with their
semblance of life: 'Et, brusquement, le nez s'aplatit, les lèvres se
détachèrent, montrant des dents blanches. La tête du noyé éclata de
rire' (p.125). Camille's corpse is no exception: 'Ce pauvre corps,
grandi entre des couvertures chaudes, grelottait sur la dalle froide'
(p.130). Pruriently, Laurent seeks out the naked females: 'il prenait
un plaisir étrange à regarder la mort violente en face, dans ses
attitudes lugubrement bizarres et grotesques. Ce spectacle l'amusait,
surtout lorsqu'il y avait des femmes étalant leur gorge nue. Ces
nudités brutalement étendues, tachées de sang, trouées par endroits,
l'attiraient et le retenaient' (p.126). His fascination with a particular
female body borders on necrophilia: 'elle souriait à demi, la tête un
peu penchée, et tendait la poitrine d'une façon provocante; on aurait

dit une courtisane vautrée (...). Laurent la regarda longtemps, promenant ses regards sur sa chair, absorbé dans une sorte de désir peureux' (p.126). Zola reflects darkly on the part played by the Morgue in the education of sexually-aware adolescents: 'ils apprenaient le vice à l'école de la mort. C'est à la Morgue que les jeunes voyous ont leur première maîtresse' (p.128).

The foregrounding of characterial responses effectively elicits the reader's own fearful reactions to the horrors of the Morgue. The repeatedly-evoked cold, wet slabs of the Morgue recall, in a poetic unity, the dank shop in the Passage du Pont-Neuf where Thérèse felt all but entombed.

Throughout *Thérèse Raquin* Zola's practice belies his claims in the preface. His theoretically detached presentation becomes a highly coloured account, rich in drama and atmosphere. As a writer of considerable imagination and persuasive powers, Zola appeals not to reason, as would be the case with the author of a scientific paper, but to the emotions. He creates mood by tonal compositions steeped in linguistic impressionism, exploits traditional literary devices such as pathetic fallacy or irony, and regularly directs his reader to a particular appreciation of character or event by intrusive fore-grounding or observation.

He aims to enlist the reader's sympathy for the paralysed Mme Raquin with her 'pauvres mains' (p.136), or for Camille 'le pauvre être' (p.105), or for Laurent 'le misérable' (p.155). The appeal is perhaps most apparent in his description of Mme Raquin's distress-ing plight: 'Rien ne fut plus navrant que ce désespoir muet et immobile.(...) les yeux seuls sanglotaient, offraient un spectacle poignant' (pp.242-43).

Zola's descriptions regularly betray his moral perspective. His characters' actions are rendered as *la débauche* (pp.291, 292), *la gloutonnerie* (p.291), *l'impudence* (pp.71, 176, 243), *l'impudeur* (p.73), *la luxure* (pp.187, 291), or *le vice* (pp.288, 291), and the consequences are seen as *le châtiment* (pp.141, 252). Of Thérèse, we read, 'elle savait qu'elle faisait le mal' (p.83), and of her adultery 'les hontes de ses amours' (p.176), while her later relationships result in 'la fatigue honteuse' (p.288). A figurative rendering of illicit passion

as 'la boue sanglante des passions' (p.241), or the reflection of
Thérèse and Laurent on 'la vie de boue qu'ils avaient menée' (p.301),
or the description of Mme Raquin's faltering hand as 'la main
vengeresse' (p.249), colour the text with implied moral judgements.
Finally, Zola's observation on the selfishness of Mme Raquin's
guests as 'l'égoïsme heureux de ses hôtes' (p.136), or his comment on
the scenes following Camille's drowning as 'la sinistre comédie'
(p.113), further testify to his ubiquitous mediating presence.

The divide between public stance and private admission,
between declared intentions and creative practice, is plain to see.
That Zola was aware of the true nature of his fiction is apparent from
a letter dated 13 September 1867, where he describes *Thérèse
Raquin* as follows: 'L'oeuvre est très dramatique, très poignante, et je
compte sur un succès d'horreur' (*20*, 1, p.523). As Zola shrewdly
recognized, the novel's real attraction lies not so much in the application of realist principles as in the narrative's atmospheric qualities,
and in its frequently disturbing appeals to the imagination.

3. People

'Dans *Thérèse Raquin*, j'ai voulu
étudier des tempéraments et non des
caractères.' (Zola, Preface to *Thérèse
Raquin*, 2nd ed., 1868)

Zola's presentation of Thérèse and Laurent as individuals apparently
devoid of moral awareness had alarmed reviewers, and, in order to
answer their hostile criticisms, the author explained his conception
of the protagonists in a preface to the novel's second edition.

His portrayal of Thérèse and Laurent as physiological
specimens conditioned by environmental forces had been inspired by
the determinist theories of contemporary anthropologists and
behavioural scientists. The protagonists, governed by their instincts,
lack free will: 'J'ai choisi des personnages souverainement dominés
par leurs nerfs et leur sang, dépourvus de libre arbitre, entraînés à
chaque acte de leur vie par les fatalités de leur chair' (p.24). Bereft of
the moral dimension traditionally ascribed to fictional characters,
Thérèse and Laurent are spared feelings of guilt and remorse. These
manifestations of conscience are replaced by reactions to the nervous
system: 'ce que j'ai été obligé d'appeler leurs remords, consiste en un
simple désordre organique, en une rébellion du système nerveux
tendu à se rompre. L'âme est parfaitement absente, j'en conviens
aisément, puisque je l'ai voulu ainsi' (p.24). The question of moral
perspectives, which had taxed more than one critic, was irrelevant in
an experiment concerned with soulless human animals: 'Thérèse et
Laurent sont des brutes humaines, rien de plus' (p.24). His fiction,
Zola contended, should be more correctly judged as a scientific
treatise. *Thérèse Raquin* was no less than 'l'étude du tempérament et
des modifications profondes de l'organisme sous la pression des
milieux et des circonstances' (p.28).

For his patently rigged experiment, Zola sets up a cast of antithetical, and complementary, individuals with specific valencies. The negative elements of Camille, Mme Raquin, and her like-minded Thursday guests, are ranged against the more positively-charged Thérèse and Laurent. In order to validate his determinist thesis, the author establishes the shaping of his complementary protagonists through details of their background, temperament, and circumstances. As Henri Mitterand (*33*) has shown, the compatibility of characters is revealed in their physical features. Thérèse shares with Laurent dark, passionate eyes, thick black hair, and a healthy complexion, while the listless Camille is blue-eyed, pale and wan.

Once introduced, the participants are locked into a narrative system designed to serve Zola's illustrative purpose. The novelist does not feign ignorance of his characters' motivation; all is reviewed, analysed and, as the author would have the reader believe, presented as diagnostic data in a clinical investigation: 'J'ai simplement fait sur deux corps vivants le travail analytique que les chirurgiens font sur des cadavres' (p.25). However, Zola's method frequently amounts to an intrusive commentary on a character's thoughts and feelings, particularly in the case of the speechless Mme Raquin, and such editorializing effectively runs counter to the professed objective reporting of observed phenomena. Not for the first time, Zola's declared aims are exposed by his novelistic practice.

Thérèse

Identified by Zola's title as the focal point of the narrative, Thérèse is presented through her immediate environment as the passive occupant of the murky shop bearing her name (p.34). An ambiguous figure wreathed in shadows, she appears pale and languid, and yet her discernible features, thick black hair, dark eyes and firm bone structure (pp.34-35), signal a latent strength of personality and reveal her part-Algerian origins (p.40). As Robert Lethbridge (*31*) has shown, her portraiture, together with the presence of the cat François, suggests the influence of Manet's painting *Olympia*.

She is 'd'une santé de fer' (p.40), and her inappropriately cloistered upbringing with her sickly cousin Camille has left unspent 'toute une énergie, toute une passion qui dormaient dans sa chair assoupie' (p.40). Her sensual being finds expression in the natural world: 'seule, dans l'herbe, au bord de l'eau, elle se couchait à plat ventre comme une bête, les yeux noirs et agrandis, le corps tordu, près de bondir. Et elle restait là, pendant des heures, ne pensant à rien, mordue par le soleil, heureuse d'enfoncer ses doigts dans la terre' (p.41). As a lover, her feline qualities, 'ses souplesses de chatte' (p.88), are in evidence, while strong emotion is registered as physical sensation: 'ses mains brûlaient' (pp.89, 121).

The divorce between her natural inclinations and the social behaviour required in the middle-class Raquin family has taught Thérèse to dissemble (pp.41,43). As she explains to Laurent: '"Ils ont fait de moi une hypocrite et une menteuse...Ils m'ont étouffée dans leur douceur bourgeoise (...) ils avaient fait de moi une brute docile avec leur bienveillance molle et leur tendresse écoeurante. Alors, j'ai menti, j'ai menti toujours"' (p.75). Such well-rehearsed duplicity enables Thérèse to play to perfection her future roles as adulteress and tearful widow (pp.82, 170).

Her existence, defined by absences and negations, is cast in the image of sterility. Unfulfilled in marriage, confined to a sepulchral shop, numbed by barren monotony and exasperated by the tedium of Mme Raquin's gatherings, Thérèse is shown to be at breaking-point (p.56). This detailed exposition of her nature, formation and circumstances is essential to the author's study of temperament and adultery. Only when the cumulative effect of these negations has been registered does Zola introduce the virile, expansive Laurent, as the opportune antidote.

Thérèse's eager scrutiny of his powerful body confirms the immediate sexual attraction: 'Elle n'avait jamais vu un homme. (...) On sentait sous ses vêtements des muscles ronds et développés, tout un corps d'une chair épaisse et ferme. Et Thérèse l'examinait avec curiosité (...) éprouvant de petits frissons lorsque ses yeux rencontraient son cou de taureau' (p.58). Her dormant sensuality is released with a sexual partner infinitely more potent than her feeble husband:

'Au premier baiser, elle se révéla courtisane. Son corps inassouvi se jeta éperdument dans la volupté' (p.72).

In accordance with Zola's thesis, the murder triggers no feelings of remorse, only a shock to her nervous system, and with it, physical change: 'Elle était vieillie' (p.132). Her progressive nervous breakdown simply demonstrates the interdependence of the physiological and the psychological. A changed personality (p.142), emotional instability (pp.143, 278, 287), nightmares and hallucinations (pp.142, 159, 205) are subsequently explained as 'une sorte de détraquement nerveux' (p.159), or 'une réaction nécessaire et fatale' (p.261). Guilt-feelings are replaced by physical sensations. An uneasy conscience becomes the presence of Camille's clammy body in the marital bed (p.205).

Yet, despite Zola's references to changes to the nervous system and a patent desire to talk about conscience in any terms other than those traditionally used, Thérèse does, in effect, exhibit all the recognized signs of an acknowledged guilt. Zola makes this clear: 'elle savait qu'elle faisait le mal' (p.83). Early manifestations are found when she imagines the cat condemning her adultery (p.80), or later, when she indulges in an insincere eulogy of Camille (pp.261-69). Gradually, the physiological terminology gives way to the language of traditional guilt and remorse. Thérèse, we learn, 'avait de vagues remords, des regrets inavoués' (p.202), or 'Thérèse était prise de remords' (p.255).

Neither moves to distance herself from the crime (p.256), nor later attempts to accept full responsibility (p.262), bring the inner peace she seeks. These calculated demonstrations of remorse, self-abasement, and supplications for Mme Raquin's forgiveness, prove to be fruitless (p.264). She recognizes her transgression, pleading with Laurent to do the same: '"Ecoute (...) nous sommes de grands coupables, il faut nous repentir, si nous voulons goûter quelque tranquillité... (...) nous sommes justement punis d'avoir commis un crime horrible"' (p.266). Her desire for punishment is expressed in her masochistic relief at her husband's violence; 'elle goûtait une volupté âpre à être frappée' (p.270). Too afraid, however, to face up to the judicial consequences of her implication in Camille's murder,

she chooses suicide, but not before admitting to the life of degrada-
tion, 'la vie de boue' (p.301), which she had led.

Laurent

Zola's experiment requires Laurent to have natural affinities with
Thérèse and to be the antithesis of the feeble Camille. Accordingly,
he is conceived as a positive force. A powerfully-built farmer's son,
'un grand gaillard, carré des épaules' (p.57), he is relaxed, outgoing
and likeable. His impressive stature is registered by the appreciative
Thérèse:

> Laurent, grand, fort, le visage frais, l'étonnait. Elle
> contemplait avec une sorte d'admiration son front bas,
> planté d'une rude chevelure noire, ses joues pleines, ses
> lèvres rouges, sa face régulière, d'une beauté sanguine.
> (...) les doigts en étaient carrés; le poing ferme devait
> être énorme et aurait pu assommer un boeuf. (p.58)

Laurent's strength and physical prowess as 'un nageur intrépide, un
rameur infatigable' (p.109), are material to his drowning of Camille.

For the conventional Raquin household, Laurent represents a
challenge to cherished beliefs in filial duty and middle-class notions
of respectability and responsibility. He has dared to abandon his law
studies for the bohemian life of the artist, and he displays a callous
indifference towards his father: '"Le père mourra bien un de ces
jours"' (p.60). Yet Zola emphasizes that Laurent is essentially
unambitious and conforming: 'Au fond, c'était un paresseux, ayant
des appétits sanguins, des désirs très arrêtés de jouissances faciles et
durables' (p.60). It is his impoverished bachelor's existence which
predisposes him to Mme Raquin's hospitality, and he quickly
recognizes the advantages of 'une retraite charmante, chaude,
tranquille, pleine de paroles et d'attentions amicales' (p.65).

A cynical, calculating opportunist, Laurent has no morality
other than that of self-interest. His premeditated seduction of
Thérèse is determined solely by sexual need: 'Pour lui, Thérèse, il est

vrai, était laide, et il ne l'aimait pas; mais en somme, elle ne lui
coûterait rien' (p.68). His marriage to her is again a calculated
decision: 'il refaisait tous ses calculs d'autrefois' (p.164). The murder
of Camille is decided without reference to moral codes: 'Dans sa
logique brutale de paysan, il trouvait ce moyen excellent et naturel.
Sa prudence native lui conseillait même cet expédient rapide' (p.94).
If necessary, Laurent is prepared to kill again to protect himself; he
brutally disposes of the cat (p.281), and seriously considers doing
away with Thérèse: 'Laurent décida qu'il tuerait Thérèse, parce que
Thérèse le gênait' (p.294). Apparently oblivious to any commitment
to Thérèse, he satisfies his sexual appetite with another mistress:
'Cette femme mit un équilibre de plus dans sa vie; il l'accepta comme
un objet utile et nécessaire qui maintenait son corps en paix et en
santé; il ne sut jamais s'il l'aimait, et jamais il ne lui vint à la pensée
qu'il était infidèle à Thérèse. Il se sentait plus gras et plus heureux.
Voilà tout' (p.145).

Like Thérèse, Laurent is deemed to experience no feelings of
guilt after his crime, but he too becomes a changed personality. He
begins to experience irrational fears, nightmares, and hallucinations,
which are marked by inexplicable physical sensations (Chapter
XVII). The wound inflicted by Camille troubles him (pp.157, 280).
In marriage, his obsession with Camille is not exorcized but exacer-
bated: his victim now appearing to occupy the conjugal bed (p.205),
to possess him (p.271), or to live on in the cat, François (pp.197,
281). As with Thérèse, his guilty conscience is explained away as
'une sorte de détraquement nerveux' (p.159).

Zola attributes Laurent's nervous state to his relationship with
Thérèse. It is an example of the physiological interaction between
individuals: 'Elle avait fait pousser dans ce grand corps, gras et mou,
un système nerveux d'une sensibilité étonnante. (...) Alors eut lieu en
lui un étrange travail; les nerfs se développèrent, l'emportèrent sur
l'élément sanguin, et ce fait seul modifia sa nature' (p.200). This
change, Zola insists, is simply physiological in nature, and has
nothing to do with conscience: 'Ses remords étaient purement
physiques. Son corps, ses nerfs irrités et sa chair tremblante avaient
seuls peur du noyé. Sa conscience n'entrait pour rien dans ses

terreurs, il n'avait pas le moindre regret d'avoir tué Camille' (p.201). The physiological case is again emphasized as Laurent's distress increases: 'Le corps souffrait horriblement, l'âme restait absente. Le misérable n'éprouvait pas un repentir; la passion de Thérèse lui avait communiqué un mal effroyable, et c'était tout' (p.202).

However, a moral dimension is imputed to the sudden burgeoning of Laurent's artistic talents: 'la maladie en quelque sorte morale, la nérvose dont tout son être était secoué, développait en lui un sens artistique d'une lucidité étrange' (p.229). His obsessive representations of Camille betray his deep-seated guilt (p.231). Unlike Thérèse, however, Laurent is unable to feign remorse: 'Il aurait voulu se repentir, lui aussi, jouer tout au moins la comédie du remords, pour essayer' (p.267). The once-jealous, possessive male, who killed for love, now tolerates his wife's infidelities (p.287). He is finally brought to share with Thérèse a moral awareness, as the couple die, 'songeant à la vie de boue qu'ils avaient menée' (p.301).

Camille

Thérèse's childhood partner, and later husband, is presented in a negative light. Zola provides the necessary details of Camille's nature, and of his formation.

He is physically unprepossessing: 'Il était petit, chétif, d'allure languissante; les cheveux d'un blond fade, la barbe rare, le visage couvert de taches de rousseur, il ressemblait à un enfant malade et gâté' (p.35). His troubled early years (p.38) have retarded his sexual development (p.42), and impaired his virility (p.61). His sheltered upbringing has inclined him to the safe excitement of dominoes (p.55), rather than to outdoor pleasures such as boating: 'Camille avait gardé cette épouvante que les enfants et les femmes ont pour les eaux profondes' (p.109). Denied an education by his overprotective mother, he is ill-prepared for adult life: 'Camille resta ignorant, et son ignorance mit comme une faiblesse de plus en lui' (p.38). He has developed into an immature, self-centred individual: 'Les tendresses, les dévouements de sa mère lui avaient donné un égoïsme féroce' (p.39). When denied his own way, he reveals his spoilt, manipulative nature: 'il la [Mme Raquin] menaça de tomber malade, si elle ne cédait pas à son caprice' (p.45).

Early patterns of domination are repeated in his adult life. An inadequate male, he is fascinated by the experiences of the more confident Laurent (p.61), and he naïvely chides Thérèse for her apparent coolness towards his admired colleague (p.82). He basks in the vicarious status of working for a large organization (p.58) and enjoys the reflected glory of having Thérèse for a wife (p.101).

In death, Camille makes a far greater impact than when alive. The horrific description of his rotting corpse in the Morgue (p.129) heralds the new, potent role he is to play in the lives of Laurent and Thérèse. As the source of their hallucinations and nightmares, he enjoys an ubiquitous presence, appearing now as a clammy bed-fellow (p.205), now in the form of the cat, François (p.197), now in every canvas Laurent paints (p.231). When the guilt-ridden Thérèse recalls him as a perfect husband (pp.267-69), he becomes a powerful instrument of torture, with the effect that Laurent feels completely taken over by Camille (p.271). Through his permanence in the minds of his murderers, Camille moves from a peripheral position in the narrative to occupy centre-stage.

Mme Raquin

An overprotective and manipulative mother, Mme Raquin is destined to play a tragically ironical role. Instrumental in stunting Camille's development, and in repressing Thérèse's natural instincts, she contrives the couple's ill-matched union, believing it to be advantageous to her sickly son: 'elle se disait que la jeune fille serait une garde vigilante auprès de Camille' (p.42). She deludes herself that the dismal shop is 'une perle, un trou délicieux' (p.47), and that her future happiness has been secured. She innocently informs Laurent that Thérèse is not as unfriendly as she perhaps first appears: '"Ne faites pas attention à la froideur de ma nièce. Je la connais; son visage paraît froid, mais son coeur est chaud de toutes les tendresses et de tous les dévouements"' (p.97). When it comes to Thérèse's proposed remarriage with Laurent, Mme Raquin is again cruelly blinded by self-interest: 'elle vit d'un coup tous les avantages qu'elle retirerait personnellement du mariage de Thérèse et de Laurent' (p.172). Ignorant of the true situation, she readily sanctions this unholy alliance (p.170), claiming Laurent as a second son (p.172), meeting his wedding expenses (p.179), and providing a handsome dowry for Thérèse (p.178). Her contentment is sadly ill-founded: 'Mme Raquin était heureuse, heureuse des soins et de l'affection de ses chers enfants' (p.238).

However, she also introduces a note of pathos into the narrative. Her heart-felt grief at Camille's loss (p.118), and her ever-present memories of him (p.169), throw into stark relief the selfish reactions of the other characters. As the helpless victim of her son's murderers, she is obliged to endure Thérèse's self-castigation (p.263), her ingratiating attention (p.264), and her dishonest eulogies of Camille (p.269). Yet she also has to suffer the couple's gratuitous cruelty (pp.243, 274, 283), while Laurent's inhuman killing of François brings her further pain and grief (p.282).

The shock of Camille's death produces a painful physical deterioration. Zola marks the phases, 'Il lui fallait une canne' (p.133); 'ne pouvant plus marcher' (p.180); 'impotente, pouvant à peine descendre à la boutique' (p.215); 'elle devenait une chose' (p.220). With the realization that Camille was murdered, she becomes totally incapacitated: 'Elle se trouvait frappée de mutisme et d'immobilité' (p.233). Only her eyes offer a sign of life, '[ses] yeux seuls bougeaient' (p.234), and, in their dramatic change, they demonstrate the physiological effects of trauma: 'Ses yeux, si doux d'ordinaire, étaient devenus noirs et durs, pareils à des morceaux de métal' (p.240).

Despite her crippled state, Mme Raquin remains a shaping force within the narrative. Her fixed, accusing stare haunts the criminals, placing them under a constant pressure, while her powerful, silent presence triggers both Laurent's brutality (p.243), and Thérèse's remorse (p.262). She brings considerable suspense to the narrative with her fruitless attempt at denouncing the guilty couple (p.248), and she stubbornly prolongs her own unhappy life to ensure their punishment (p.274). She is also the silent witness to the growing antagonism. She derives a certain pleasure from observing Laurent's violence towards Thérèse: 'Une joie ardente luisait dans ses yeux, lorsque Laurent levait sa large main sur la tête de Thérèse' (p.259). Finally, with gloating satisfaction, she watches them die, 'les écrasant de regards lourds' (p.301).

Secondary figures

The Thursday guests, Michaud, Grivet, Olivier and Suzanne, act as barometers for the moods of Thérèse and occasionally further the plot. As a group, 'ces créatures grotesques et sinistres' (p.55) are inward-looking (p.63), and only serve to exacerbate Thérèse's sense of frustration and boredom: 'Toutes ces têtes-là l'exaspéraient' (p.55). The Thursday gatherings are evenings to be endured, not enjoyed.

The married couple, Olivier and Suzanne, represent the conformity and complacency Thérèse is desperate to escape from in her own marriage. Initially, Suzanne, 'toute pâle, les yeux vagues, les lèvres blanches, le visage mou' (p.55), is of little interest, but after the murder, she becomes welcome company (pp.218, 276). Similarly, the retired police inspector Michaud, and the administrator Grivet, are at first nothing but a source of irritation: 'Le vieux Michaud étalait une face blafarde, tachée de plaques rouges, une de ces faces mortes de vieillard tombé en enfance; Grivet avait le masque étroit, les yeux ronds, les lèvres minces d'un crétin' (p.55). Their conversation is always the same: 'Michaud racontait toujours les mêmes histoires de meurtre et de vol; Grivet parlait en même temps de ses employés, de ses chefs, de son administration' (p.85). However, as the situation between Thérèse and Laurent becomes unbearable, their presence becomes indispensable: 'Si Michaud et Grivet n'étaient pas venus, elle serait allée les chercher' (pp.219-20).

These two characters do have a part to play in the unfolding of the plot. The retired police inspector's revelation that many murderers escape detection (p.98) prompts Laurent to dispose of Camille. It is again through Michaud that Thérèse and Laurent succeed in promoting the idea of their marriage. In this matter, self-interest motivates the former inspector, for without the marriage his cherished Thursday gatherings might cease (p.214).

The naïve and platitudinous Grivet is a perfect agent for Zola's irony. His interventions, whether his 'plaisanteries épicées' (p.177) at the wedding, or his allusions to Thérèse and Laurent starting a family (p.183), prove to be pointedly inappropriate. He crassly attributes the lethargy of the haunted Thérèse and Laurent to nights of passion: 'il les plaisantait, il demandait à quand le baptême' (p.221), and his sentimental reference to the couple as 'les tourtereaux' (p.221), only serves to highlight the grim reality of their unhappy marriage. He is instrumental in the most cruel of ironies concerning Mme Raquin's attempt to expose her son's murderers. In his overweening self-confidence, he triumphantly misrepresents her unfinished denunciation as an expression of her gratitude (p.250). True to form, on the eve of the double suicide, he naïvely styles the strife-torn Raquin household, 'le Temple de la Paix' (p.298).

As human beings, Zola's creations have little to recommend them. With the exception of Laurent's considerate friend, the unnamed painter, they are all fundamentally selfish, calculating, and unscrupulous. They are, in Zola's terms, expressions of a given temperament and the shaping forces of a given environment. Though theoretically denied free will, the main characters do make choices, albeit bad ones, and do exhibit a moral awareness, even if it is necessarily expressed in physiological terms. The stipulated objective presentation escapes Zola. He regularly foregrounds his characters, intervenes to comment and, most obviously, passes moral judgement. In his portrayal of the speechless Mme Raquin, his method is put to the severest test, as he regularly needs to attribute thoughts and feelings to her. Her existence as a silent witness confirms her conception as a function of Zola's narrative design. An examination of the novel's structure will throw further light on the author's manipulation of character to bring about the predetermined outcome of his theoretically open-ended experiment.

4. Narrative Structure

'L'affabulation se simplifie (...)'
(Zola, *Deux définitions du roman*,
1866)

In his paper on the evolution of the novel genre, Zola had dismissed sensational, convoluted plots as outmoded. The new generation of scientifically-inspired writers, he argued, was more concerned with deriving a logically coherent narrative structure from the evidence of their documentary investigations: 'Il ne s'agit plus d'inventer une histoire compliquée d'une invraisemblance dramatique qui étonne le lecteur; il s'agit uniquement d'enregistrer des faits humains, de montrer à nu le mécanisme du corps et de l'âme. L'affabulation se simplifie (...)' (*21*, 10, p.281). Useful insights into the relationship between the individual and society could be derived from an informed, analytically-based presentation: 'Il [l'auteur] procède comme nos chimistes et nos mathématiciens; il décompose les actions, en détermine les causes, en explique les résultats; il opère selon des équations fixes, ramenant les faits à l'étude de l'influence des milieux sur les individualités' (ibid., p.281).

In his preface, Zola places *Thérèse Raquin* in this category by insisting on the scientific nature of his undertaking, 'l'analyse scientifique que j'ai tenté d'appliquer' (p.28), and by defining his novel as 'l'étude du tempérament et des modifications profondes de l'organisme sous la pression des milieux et des circonstances' (p.28). He sees his role not as a creator, but rather as a clinical scientist observing the progress of an experiment on two chosen specimens: 'J'ai cherché à suivre pas à pas dans ces brutes le travail sourd des passions, les poussées de l'instinct, les détraquements cérébraux survenus à la suite d'une crise nerveuse' (p.24). The account of these fictional events is implicitly likened to a scientific research paper: 'Qu'on lise le roman avec soin, on verra que chaque chapitre est l'étude d'un cas curieux de physiologie' (p.25). These pretensions to analysis are patently untenable, since Zola can only reveal what he himself has introduced to be revealed. In practice, his declared open-ended examination is nothing more than a circumscribed demonstration of a given thesis, in which narrative elements are systematically arranged to validate his preconceived conclusion.

The story itself is far from original. A woman unfulfilled in marriage commits adultery, and is complicitous in the murder of her husband by her jealous lover. The guilty couple escape detection, are free to marry, but find no happiness in their legitimate union. Their dream turns to a nightmare of recrimination, hatred, and corrosive suspicion, culminating in the self-inflicted violence of suicide.

The originality of *Thérèse Raquin* lies in Zola's treatment. Thoroughly deterministic in concept, and highly dramatic in presentation, the novel's stage-managed action represents Zola's perception of causality, with each development in the narrative the acting-out of a particular premise.

For more than one critic,[3] the structure of *Thérèse Raquin* is essentially that of a classical tragedy. The position is most fully developed by Blandine Rickert (*35*) who in her analysis discerns a prologue, i.e. the introduction of characters (Chapters I-V); a complication, i.e. the adultery bringing the need to remove Camille (VI-X); a tragic error, i.e. the murder (XI); a reversal of expectations, i.e. the unhappy marriage (XII-XXI); and events leading to the denouement, i.e. the double suicide (XXII-XXXII). Henri Mitterand sees the shape of the novel replicating the tripartite division of the short story, with each section building towards a dramatic event: the murder, the marriage and the suicides. He further qualifies the novel as 'une tragédie, dans laquelle le déterminisme des instincts irrépressibles tient lieu de fatalité' (*32*, p.493). While reflecting, and largely confirming, these positions, our approach is to follow through Zola's declared objective of presenting a clinical case-study.

---

[3] See: Michel Claverie (*23*, pp.138-47); Henri Mitterand (*32*, pp.498-502); Janice Best (*11*, pp.43-46).

The initial requirement of his method is an exposition of the factors material to Thérèse's adultery with Laurent. This is achieved in the first four chapters where details of Thérèse's environment, both physical and human, both past and present, are recorded. The dismal shop is described, and participants in the drama introduced: Thérèse herself (p.34), Mme Raquin, Camille, and the cat François (p.35). The shop's side-entrance, which provides direct access to the bedroom, is noted (p.36). The reader's understanding of the enigmatic Thérèse is furthered by a summary of her formative years with the Raquin family at Vernon (Chapter II). This use of flashback is far from gratuitous: the looping narrative structure reflects the deterministic view that the past is the key to present, and indeed, future conduct. The revelation of her unnatural upbringing with her sickly cousin (p.40), and of the family pressures leading to her loveless marriage (p.42), explains her depression and resentment.

The action is returned to Paris. Thérèse's monotonous existence in the shop is adduced as the cause of her splenetic lethargy (III, IV). Details of Camille's employment as a clerk (p.49) prepare the introduction of his colleagues, Grivet and Laurent. Temporal references emphasize the empty, dreary existence endured by Thérèse, who finds herself trapped in a situation not unlike that of Emma Bovary: 'Pendant trois ans, les jours se suivirent et se ressemblèrent. Camille ne s'absenta pas une seule fois de son bureau; sa mère et sa femme sortirent à peine de la boutique. Thérèse (...) voyait la vie s'étendre devant elle, toute nue, amenant chaque soir la même couche froide et chaque matin la même journée vide' (pp.50-51). The introduction of the secondary figures, Michaud (p.53), Grivet, Olivier, and Suzanne (p.54), and of the ritual Thursday gatherings with their fatuous games and mindless tittle-tattle (pp.55-56), completes the exposition of the negative forces shaping Thérèse's life. By this stage she has become dangerously volatile.

Zola triggers the experiment by adding Laurent to the existing narrative formula. The Thursday gatherings provide the means for his assimilation, and the focus narrows to this specific occasion (p.57). In Zola's experimental terms, Laurent has the particular chemical valency to combine with Thérèse's latent properties.

Contrasting with the colourless Camille, the expansive newcomer produces an immediate reaction in Thérèse (p.58). Whereas each of the previous chapters has closed with a statement of her depression, Chapter V records a different mood, as Zola notes the first results in his clinical trial: 'La nature sanguine de ce garçon, sa voix pleine, ses rires gras, les senteurs âcres et puissantes qui s'échappaient de sa personne, troublaient la jeune femme et la jetaient dans une sorte d'angoisse nerveuse' (p.63).

Zola prepares the next stage of his experiment by reviewing Laurent's nature and circumstances. Laurent finds Mme Raquin's hospitality attractive because of his own meagre existence in cramped rooms (p.63). These same rooms will witness the decision to murder Camille (p.89) and, for a Laurent gripped by fear, undergo an expressionistic transformation (p.149). Laurent's self-interested offer to paint Camille's portrait sets up the opportunity to seduce Thérèse (p.69). The unflattering portrait, 'le visage de Camille ressemblait à la face verdâtre d'un noyé' (p.69), becomes an important structural unit in Zola's narrative, both anticipating the victim's violent end (p.112), and giving rise to Laurent's hallucinations on his wedding night (p.194).

With the foregrounding statement 'les amants trouvèrent leur liaison nécessaire, fatale, toute naturelle' (p.71), Zola presents the affair as the inevitable outcome of frustration and the couple's particular sexual compatibility (pp.72-73). In a dramatic recapitulation of the details given in Chapters II and III, the narrative loops back on itself, as a now liberated Thérèse pours out her resentment about her repressed upbringing and her joyless marriage (pp.73-75). This intimate rehearsal increases identification with Thérèse, while distancing the reader still further from Camille.

The overwhelming force of the passion gripping the adulterous couple is demonstrated by the risks they are prepared to run. At any moment they could be betrayed by neighbouring shopkeepers (p.72), or surprised by Mme Raquin as, indeed, is nearly the case (p.78). The tension they experience in their risky affair is exteriorized in the whimsical notion that the cat François would denounce them, if only he had the power of speech (p.79). Later this fantasy assumes more sinister resonances when, after Camille's death, Laurent comes to believe that François does indeed have such powers and intentions (p.292).

Zola the analyst reviews the factors which have led to the couple's mutual attraction: 'La nature et les circonstances semblaient avoir fait cette femme pour cet homme, et les avoir poussés l'un vers l'autre. A eux deux, la femme, nerveuse et hypocrite, l'homme, sanguin et vivant en brute, ils faisaient un couple puissamment lié' (p.83). Their relationship continues undisturbed for some eight months (p.85), but in Laurent's apprehension, 'la (...) crainte de voir cesser cette belle existence' (p.86), Zola already points to the next phase of the experimental programme.

The eventual refusal of Laurent's employer to grant afternoon leave (p.87) precipitates the anticipated crisis. Laurent's sexual needs must be satisfied: 'Il y avait quinze jours que Laurent ne pouvait approcher de Thérèse. Alors il sentit combien cette femme lui était devenue nécessaire; l'habitude de la volupté lui avait créé des appétits nouveaux, d'une exigence aiguë' (p.88). An evening meeting contrived at his rooms (p.89) only serves to persuade the lovers that Camille, as the major impediment to their pleasure, must be removed (p.90). In much the same way that Zola set out the circumstances which led to Thérèse and Laurent becoming lovers, the author now charts the path by which they become murderers.

Laurent's homicidal intentions attract the clinical observation required of the serious analytical novelist : 'Et c'est ainsi qu'un nouveau coin de sa nature inconsciente venait de se révéler: il s'était mis à rêver l'assassinat dans les emportements de l'adultère' (p.93). Cruel ironies are prepared in Laurent's desire to have Thérèse to himself for the whole night (p.90), and especially in his self-persuasion that the murder will procure peace of mind: 'Il tuait afin de vivre calme et heureux' (p.94). A tormented, unconsummated wedding night (p.188), and an intolerable existence with Thérèse will be his reward.

In narrative terms, the unspoken agreement to kill Camille generates tension and suspense. No plan is specified, and a third party is required to precipitate events. In ironical vein, Zola draws on the former police officer Michaud to firm up Laurent's intention, with a timely revelation that many murderers escape detection (p.98). This authoritative information helps to seal Camille's fate. Laurent's unresolved sexual frustration is also adduced: 'Depuis un mois, il vivait dans une chasteté pleine de colère' (p.104). These pressures, coupled with Michaud's intervention, turn the possibility of murder into a probability and, given favourable circumstances, this probability into a certainty. Zola introduces the episode of the boating trip to provide precisely these circumstances.

Since it is the author's experimental aim to trace the effect of given stimuli on Thérèse and Laurent, it is they, and not their victim, who remain the focus of interest. After Mme Raquin's characteristic forebodings (p.103), tension rises with the indication of Laurent's sexual desire; 'il regardait avec des yeux fauves les balancements de hanches de sa maîtresse' (p.103), and increases as he contemplates violence against the dozing Camille (p.105). Reference back to Michaud's disclosure tightens the strands of the plot, and confirms Laurent's decision to remove his rival: 'Il voulait se débarrasser de Camille uniquement pour épouser Thérèse: il entendait vivre au soleil, après le crime, comme le meurtrier du roulier, dont le vieux Michaud avait conté l'histoire' (p.106). The murder is duly committed (p.112), but in Zola's scheme it is this criminal solution which creates the problems. The wound inflicted on Laurent's neck and the failure to find Camille's body give rise to further narrative developments. Dramatic intensity is maintained as the news of the drowning is communicated to other characters, and in particular to a grief-stricken Mme Raquin (p.117). The pace slackens over the next three chapters (XIII, XIV, XV) where, in a progressive opening-out of the narrative, the impact of Camille's death is observed on Laurent, Mme Raquin, Thérèse, and the Thursday guests.

Laurent discovers that, far from relegating Camille to oblivion, he has given him an importance he never enjoyed when alive. Once driven to distraction by Camille's unwelcome existence, Laurent is now preoccupied by his disturbing absence. A new pressure on the character is thus built into the narrative. Suspense mounts with each fruitless visit to the Morgue, and the first of many nightmares results (p.126), though none, as yet, is directly associated with Camille. Thérèse and Mme Raquin reveal emotional strain: Thérèse is deemed to have aged from the shock (p.132), while in Mme Raquin the first stages of physical deterioration are observed (p.133). Finally, the reactions of the Thursday group are relayed. Shock is mingled with a selfish concern that Camille's death could end their cosy gatherings.

With the immediate repercussions of the murder noted, the reactions of the protagonists during the fifteen-month period of mourning are examined. Zola again foregrounds his clinical approach, and thus the framework for the next section of his narrative: 'Et, dans les commencements, Laurent et Thérèse se laissèrent aller à l'existence nouvelle qui les transformait; il se fit en eux un travail sourd qu'il faudrait analyser avec une délicatesse extrême, si l'on voulait en marquer toutes les phases' (p.139). A reorientation of the narrative line seems likely when Laurent considers marrying his new mistress (p.145), but, given Zola's closed system, this potential development is inevitably curtailed (p.146). Attention reverts to Laurent's relationship with Thérèse.

The couple's decision to pursue their marriage-plans brings about horrific nightmares. Laurent experiences hallucinations shaped from his memories of Camille at the Morgue, and, in a narrative development more readily understood in terms of traditional symbolism rather than clinical observation, the scar on his neck begins to vex him (pp.153, 157, 192, 280, etc.). Thérèse, as his accomplice, simultaneously experiences identical nightmares. This phenomenon, Zola insists, is consistent with previous clinical findings: 'Ils eurent dès lors un seul corps et une seule âme pour jouir et pour souffrir. Cette communauté, cette pénétration mutuelle est un fait de psychologie et de physiologie qui a souvent lieu chez les êtres que de grandes secousses nerveuses heurtent violemment l'un à l'autre' (pp.159-60).

The cure for these shared nervous disorders is assumed to lie in the long-delayed marriage, but this must be achieved without arousing suspicions. Zola again deploys Michaud as a catalyst to persuade the interested parties of the advantages of such a union (pp.168-77). Further narrative openings are prepared by Mme Raquin's financial settlement on the couple (p.178). Marriage however, like the murder, proves to be a false solution, bringing not union but disintegration. The downward spiral accelerates as expectations are comprehensively reversed. The narrative again arches back on itself as the two hesitant lovers find themselves once more in the room of their adulterous raptures. Shared intimacies are recalled, and Laurent's personal version of the already-narrated Morgue visits parallels the earlier dramatic retelling by Thérèse of her life with Camille (p.194). A misrepresentation of these events highlights the couple's stress. Camille, through his portrait, becomes a haunting presence (p.194), and his assumed attempts to enter the marital chamber by the side-door (p.196) is an ironical recall of Laurent's adulterous visits. The realization that the visitor is none other than the cat François now reawakens the old fears of betrayal. For Laurent, the cat and Camille merge into a single being (p.197), and this delusion leads to his savage destruction of the animal (p.282), in what amounts to a symbolic re-enactment of Camille's murder.

After dramatizing the couple's distress, Zola reverts to commentary: La nature sèche et nerveuse de Thérèse avait agi d'une façon bizarre sur la nature épaisse et sanguine de Laurent' (p.199). The novelist's physiological observation leads to the next phase of his clinical investigation: 'Il serait curieux d'étudier les changements qui se produisent parfois dans certains organismes, à la suite de circonstances déterminées' (p.200). Now less dependent on external events, the narrative is more concerned with exposing mental states. The conviction that Camille has a material presence in the marital bed (p.207) is symptomatic of the protagonists' anguish. Their world seems to have been turned on its head. The Raquin shop, once a desirable haven for Laurent, has become his torture chamber (p.216), while for Thérèse, the shop's previously depressing tomb-like atmosphere is now enjoyed (p.218). The formerly despised Thursday guests are now welcomed as a comforting diversion, and the presence of Mme Raquin is recognized as indispensable: 'Ils ne voulaient pas perdre un tiers qui leur rendait les soirées supportables' (p.220). The dread of remaining alone together is identified as a potential pressure point, and this situation awaits exploitation in the narrative scheme.

To illustrate posited links between trauma and creativity, Zola contrives the episode in which Laurent uses Thérèse's dowry (p.178) to return to his life as a painter (Chapter XXV). The unnamed fellow artist from his past (p.59) is duly brought back to register the dramatic transformation in Laurent's talents (p.288), while the omniscient narrator reflects: 'Sans doute un phénomène étrange s'était accompli dans l'organisme du meurtrier de Camille. Il est difficile à l'analyse de pénétrer à de telles profondeurs' (pp.228-29). With the unhappy perception that all his work contains images of his victim, a despairing Laurent destroys his canvasses to bring the episode to an abrupt close (p.232).

Zola steps up the pressure on his protagonists with the feared advent of Mme Raquin's total incapacity: 'Dès ce jour, la vie des époux devint intolérable' (p.234). Their consequential unguarded quarrelling reveals the truth of Camille's murder to a devastated Mme Raquin. She now becomes a potential threat to their freedom, and her attempt to denounce them is prepared (p.239). Grivet's claim to enjoy a telepathic understanding with her is used to produce the tense and ironical episode in which he confidently misrepresents her message (pp.247-50). The closed narrative scheme precludes the possibility of her success as an alternative resolution to the drama.

The protagonists' path to self-destruction is repeatedly sign-posted in Zola's account of their deepening hostility: 'La haine devait forcément venir' (p.251). Their impossible marriage is seen as poetic justice, as 'le châtiment fatal du meurtre' (p.25), and their end is ominously predicted as 'un dénouement sinistre et violent' (p.252). The narrative again turns back on itself as the couple dispute responsibility for their predicament (pp.257-59).

Zola returns to the language of the clinical observer: 'Une nouvelle phase se déclara' (p.261). Thérèse's lachrymose self-castigation is seen as 'une réaction nécessaire et fatale' (p.261). Her attempts to distance herself from the crime entail a misrepresentation of her unhappy life with Camille, while Laurent's preferred memory of his role in Camille's death is no less a distortion of the facts (p.267). With the protagonists reworking the past, the strictly chronological structure gives way to the psychological, as present attitudes to earlier events assume greater importance.

In Zola's exploration of the couple's descent into mutual loathing, several narrative openings are again implied: Mme Raquin's attempted suicide (pp.273-74); a formal separation for the protagonists (p.275); Thérèse's potential motherhood (p.278). Each opening is quickly foreclosed. In Zola's unified system, the characters are held to the pre-ordained path, and the omniscient observer again signals the inexorable progress of the experiment: 'le dénouement ne pouvait être loin' (pp.274-75). The pattern of ironical reversals is maintained as pressures on Laurent increase. He now grows ever more frustrated by the life of leisure he had once coveted: 'La paresse, cette existence de brute qu'il avait rêvée, était son châtiment' (p.279). The scar on his neck is a constant irritant: 'Il portait ainsi partout avec lui le souvenir vivant et dévorant de son crime' (p.280). The cat François is returned to the narrative (p.281) to become the focus of Laurent's tensions, and his cruel killing of the family pet (p.281) marks his ever-deepening depravity.

Narrative tension is maintained by the guilty couple's mutual suspicion of an impending betrayal to the police (p.286). Laurent's indifference to Thérèse's debauchery further signals the moral decline of a once-jealous man who had killed his rival (p.287). His own failed excursions into sexual adventure (p.291) contrast sharply with his earlier enjoyment of a mistress during Thérèse's mourning.

The final working-through of Zola's posited physiological equation brings hatred and madness in the wake of mistrust: 'A la haine vint se joindre la méfiance, la méfiance acheva de les rendre fous' (p.293). Now united in mutual fear and mistrust, rather than in passion, Thérèse and Laurent have, ironically, never been closer: 'Jamais, depuis leur mariage, ils n'avaient vécu si étroitement liés l'un à l'autre, et jamais ils n'avaient tant souffert' (p.294). The consequences of the murder become terminal, with each partner seeking to end the life of the other (p.296). As a prelude to this final act, Zola assembles the other members of his cast. The crass

Thursday group remains convinced of the couple's marital bliss. Only the paralysed hostess anticipates the impending violence: 'elle laissa agir les conséquences de l'assassinat de Camille qui devaient tuer les assassins à leur tour' (p.298), and triumphantly she witnesses the double suicide of her son's murderers (p.300).

For Zola, the originality of his particular version of the famous court case lay in a narration shaped according to the principles of scientific inquiry. According to his own precepts, he begins by setting out the essential characteral and environmental data. He then notes the interaction of his physiological specimens, or fictional beings, and charts the sequence of events triggered by the pressures to which they are subjected. The scientific truth of his experiment, that is, the illusion of inevitability, is derived from the coherence of his demonstration. To reproduce this effect, his documentary narrative structure must be seen to evolve logically from the implications of the events portrayed. Absent in theory, but coexistent in practice, are traditional literary features which enrich the structure with a poetic, and frequently ironical, patterning. Zola's pseudo-scientific fictional experiment, narrated through each of its discrete stages, betrays at every twist and intervention the presence of the literary practitioner masquerading as the clinical scientist.

5. The Horror Story

> 'Il est certain que, dans *Thérèse Raquin*, les choses sont poussées au cauchemar' (Zola, *Le Messager de l'Europe*, October 1879)

Contemporary reviewers were right: *Thérèse Raquin* is a horror story. From the outset, Zola recognized that his fiction was rather more than a dispassionate case-study of adultery and murder, and had confided to his publisher: 'je compte sur un succès d'horreur' (*20*, 1, p.523). As several critics[4] have argued, *Thérèse Raquin*, both in substance and form, can be identified with the *roman noir* or Gothic novel.

The genre was characterized by a fascination with the abnormal and the inexplicable. Strange happenings, disturbing hallucinations, and nightmares with their own absurd logic, were recounted in suitably unnerving terms. In this respect, the influence of Edgar Allan Poe, whose stories had been translated by Baudelaire in 1856-57, cannot be discounted. Through his own extraordinary tale of guilt and fear, of neurosis and nightmare, of hauntings and hallucinations, Zola places *Thérèse Raquin* within this current of horror fiction.

Tonality

In the twisted world of the horror story where appearances deceive, where expectations are inevitably reversed, and where naïveté is a

---

[4] See: Lilian R. Furst (*28*, pp.189-202); Chantal Jennings (*30*, pp.94-101); John Lapp (*18*, pp.88-120).

fatal flaw, dramatic irony has a ready-made role. People and situations are never quite as they first appear. For Zola, the peace of an
autumn evening heralds a violent murder; a happy social gathering is
the prelude to a double suicide. An apparently unemotional woman
is a creature of passion; a retired policeman unwittingly encourages
homicide. A murder committed to ensure peace and happiness brings
only torment and misery. The dream of two lovers to be inseparable
becomes a shared nightmare of an intolerable life together. In such
elements lies the cruel, ironical perspective of Zola's tale of adultery
and murder.

The narrative is punctuated by extreme situations designed to
inspire feelings of terror or revulsion. Zola's assault on the senses
can be direct, with deliberately shocking detail, as in his presentation
of Camille's putrescent corpse at the Morgue (p.129), or his account
of Thérèse's dread of an unwanted pregnancy and the miscarriage
she provokes: 'Elle avait vaguement peur d'accoucher d'un noyé. Il
lui semblait sentir dans ses entrailles le froid d'un cadavre dissous et
amolli' (p.278).

An unnerving emotional pitch is created, and sustained,
through Zola's knowing exploitation of a highly-charged vocabulary.
He deploys, often to melodramatic excess, adjectives such as
sinistre, *atroce* or *ignoble*, and nouns such as *crise*, *angoisse*, *effroi*
or *terreur* to produce his disturbing effects. Perhaps even more
disquieting, however, are the veiled allusions to scenes of raw
emotion. The erotic intimacies of Thérèse and Laurent are left to the
imagination: 'dans la chambre nue et glaciale, se passaient des scènes
de passion ardentes, d'une brutalité sinistre' (p.77). Later, the violent
consequences of their mutual loathing are similarly unspecified:
'C'étaient des scènes atroces, des étouffements, des coups, des cris
ignobles, des brutalités honteuses' (p.253).

The nightmarish mood of the narrative is largely determined
by repeated evocations of cold, dank places with allusions to
constriction and violence. The initial description of the arcade carries
intimations of murderous acts (pp.32-33), while images of confine-
ment govern the existence of both Thérèse (pp.40, 276) and Laurent,
whose cramped flat 'ressemblait à un trou, à un caveau creusé dans

une argile grise' (pp.225-26). The presentation of the shop as cold and damp (pp.35, 51) anticipates the tonal elements in the accounts of the drowning (p.111), and of the Morgue (p.205), while the imagined presence of Camille in the marital bed, 'le corps humide (...) leur glaçait la chair' (p.205), extends the metaphorical coldness into a chilling psychological reality.

Gothic images of premature burial render Thérèse's numbed reaction to the sepulchral shop (pp.47, 75), and the presence of the lifeless Thursday guests seems to confirm her impression: 'parfois des hallucinations la prenaient, elle se croyait enfouie au fond d'un caveau, en compagnie de cadavres mécaniques' (pp.55-56). Following the murder, her depression deepens, and the image of burial returns; 'elle devenait triste à mourir au fond de ce caveau sombre, puant le cimetière' (p.276). The decay and putrefaction of death are evoked: 'elle laissait le magasin se pourrir, elle abandonnait les marchandises à la poussière et à l'humidité. Des odeurs de moisi traînaient, des araignées descendaient du plafond' (p.276). Her illusion of entombment grows more macabre and seems to draw on Baudelairean images of spleen: 'elle s'imaginait qu'elle venait d'être enterrée vive (...) au fond d'une fosse commune où grouillaient des morts' (p.218), and this sensation is increased by the presence of the cadaverous Suzanne, 'souriant d'un sourire pâle, vivant à demi, mettant dans la boutique une fade senteur de cimetière' (p.218).

Images of catalepsy and premature burial reminiscent of Poe are again deployed to conjure up Mme Raquin's feelings of impotent frustration when she discovers the truth about her son's death: 'Ses sensations ressemblaient à celles d'un homme tombé en léthargie qu'on enterrerait et qui, bâillonné par les liens de sa chair, entendrait sur sa tête le bruit sourd des pelletées de sable' (pp.240-41). Allusions to darkness and coldness complete the evocation of the grave: 'il lui semblait qu'elle tombait dans un trou noir et froid' (pp.241-42).

Lighting effects, too, form an integral part of the novel's tonal structure. At key moments, atmospheric lighting dramatically foregrounds people and places. The dim and strangely-refracted natural light in the shopping arcade distorts the appearance of the goods on display (p.34), while by night the murky, gas-lit arcade resembles a catacomb (p.33). Perceived through the yellow light of the smoking lamp, the Thursday guests appear to Thérèse like phantasmagoria: 'elle les voyait à travers une sorte de brouillard jaune et fumeux qui sortait de la lampe' (p.55), and in the uncertain light of a match, the panic-stricken Laurent finds reality alarmingly distorted (p.150).

Camille's death is prefigured in Zola's poetic rendering of the dusk (p.110), while the blood-red flames of the fire betray the faces of his murderers: 'Par instants, des jets de flammes rougeâtres s'échappaient du bois, et alors des reflets sanglants couraient sur le visage des meurtriers' (p.186).

For Mme Raquin's dramatic attempt at denouncing the criminals, the lamp becomes a theatrical spotlight, focusing attention on her hand: 'Thérèse (...) regardait la main de sa tante, blafarde sous la lumière crue de la lampe, comme une main vengeresse' (p.247), and for the final melodramatic scene of the double suicide, the lamp serves a similar function, now drawing attention to the bodies: 'Les cadavres restèrent toute la nuit sur le carreau de la salle à manger, tordus, vautrés, éclairés de lueurs jaunâtres par les clartés de la lampe que l'abat-jour jetait sur eux' (p.301).

Hallucinations and nightmares

If for Mme Raquin life has become a metaphorical nightmare — 'il lui semblait qu'elle était perdue dans un rêve d'horreur qui n'aurait pas de fin' (p.254) — for her son's killers, nightmares and hallucinations are only too real. Laurent's attempts to usurp Camille's place in marriage bring sleepless nights and horrendous illusions as the dead husband returns to torment his murderers.

For Laurent, normality is subverted by irrational fears and ghastly hallucinations. Zola conveys the murderer's feelings of foreboding and terror by exploiting commonly-held fears of the dark and of the supernatural. Dreadful premonitions make him reluctant to return to his rooms alone: 'Un effroi d'enfant, inexplicable, imprévu, lui fit craindre de trouver un homme caché dans sa mansarde' (p.149). The dark passage and stairs become places of previously unsuspected evil: 'Cette allée, ce bout d'escalier, d'un noir terrible, l'épouvantaient. (...) il se disait qu'il y avait peut-être (...) des assassins qui lui sauteraient brusquement à la gorge quand il passerait' (p.150). A nightmare feeling of helplessness is evoked as he stands petrified in the dark, sensing the presence of others, but unable to strike a match to see: 'L'allumette s'éteignit. Il resta immobile, haletant, n'osant s'enfuir, frottant les allumettes sur le mur humide avec une anxiété qui faisait trembler sa main. Il lui semblait entendre des voix, des bruits de pas devant lui. Les allumettes se brisaient entre les doigts' (p.150). Feelings of suspended panic are conveyed as the match finally, slowly, begins to give some light, bringing not relief but only increased fear: 'Le soufre se mit à bouillir, à enflammer le bois avec une lenteur qui redoubla les angoisses de Laurent; dans la clarté pâle et bleuâtre du soufre, dans les lueurs vacillantes qui couraient, il crut distinguer des formes monstrueuses' (p.150).

His room holds further terrors. Attempts at sleep bring only alarming hallucinations based on his desire for Thérèse, while the wound inflicted by Camille conjures up the presence of his victim: 'il lui sembla que sa couche était étrangement secouée; il s'imagina que Camille se trouvait caché sous le lit, et que c'était lui qui le remuait ainsi, pour le faire tomber et le mordre' (p.153). Laurent's fear produces physical reactions: 'les dents claquant de peur' (p.153), 'les cheveux dressés sur la tête' (p.153). Happy dreams of meeting his mistress are transformed into macabre nightmares in which Camille replaces Thérèse: 'Mais au lieu de Thérèse, au lieu de la jeune femme en jupon, la gorge nue, ce fut Camille qui lui ouvrit, Camille tel qu'il l'avait vu à la Morgue, verdâtre, atrocement défiguré. Le cadavre lui tendait les bras, avec un rire ignoble, en montrant un bout de langue noirâtre dans la blancheur de ses dents' (p.154). In his waking moments, Laurent experiences horrendous hallucinations: 'par moments, des terreurs l'aplatissaient contre la terre humide; il lui semblait voir, sous l'arche du pont, passer de longues traînées de noyés qui descendaient au fil du courant' (p.162). Thérèse, too, suffers similar imaginings, and, with a traditional image of hell-fire,

Zola conveys the couple's nightly torments: 'Chaque nuit, le noyé les visitait, l'insomnie les couchait sur un lit de charbons ardents et les retournait avec des pinces de feu' (p.161).

The criminals' most traumatic experiences come after their marriage. Whereas previously the drowned Camille had merely appeared in grotesque nightmares or hallucinations, now he assumes a tangible presence. He joins them at the fireside: 'Le spectre de Camille évoqué venait de s'asseoir entre les nouveaux époux, en face du feu qui flambait. Thérèse et Laurent retrouvaient la senteur froide et humide du noyé dans l'air chaud qu'ils respiraient; ils se disaient qu'un cadavre était là, près d'eux' (pp.188-89). To their horror, Camille's clammy body, evil-smelling and putrescent, takes up position in the marital bed to form a physical and psychological barrier: 'C'était comme un obstacle ignoble qui les séparait. (...) et cet obstacle devenait matériel pour eux; ils touchaient le corps, ils le voyaient étalé, pareil à un lambeau verdâtre et dissous, ils respiraient l'odeur infecte de ce tas de pourriture humaine' (p.205).

When, through desperation rather than desire, they consummate their marriage, they find that Camille is not to be denied. The image of hell-fire returns:

> Quand leurs membres se touchèrent, ils crurent qu'ils étaient tombés sur un brasier. Ils poussèrent un cri et se pressèrent davantage, afin de ne pas laisser entre leur chair de place pour le noyé. Et ils sentaient toujours des lambeaux de Camille, qui s'écrasait ignoblement entre eux, glaçant leur peau par endroits, tandis que le reste de leur corps brûlait. (p.210)

The imagined corpse, the materialization of the couple's guilty conscience, is triumphant: 'Et, dans leurs sanglots, il leur sembla entendre les rires de triomphe du noyé' (p.212). Thereafter, Camille becomes a dominant force in the household. Thérèse's repeated, taunting eulogy of her dead husband's qualities seems to lend substance to Camille's imagined presence: 'Le cadavre, qui hantait déjà la maison, y fut introduit ouvertement. Il s'assit sur les sièges, se mit devant la table, s'étendit dans le lit, se servit des meubles, des objets qui traînaient' (p.270). Subjected to this barrage of unfavourable comparisons, Laurent is left with the uncanny impression that he has become the rival he removed: 'il s'imagina, à force d'être comparé à Camille, de se servir des objets dont Camille s'était servi, qu'il était Camille, qu'il s'identifiait avec sa victime' (p.271).

Camille's portrait

The role of Camille's portrait, and Zola's linked account of neurosis and artistic creativity, also borrow from the traditions of Gothic literature. Laurent's badly-executed canvas acquires a thematic importance in the author's depiction of an increasingly nightmarish world. The portrait clearly signals the eventual manner of the victim's death: 'Le portrait était ignoble (...) et le visage de Camille ressemblait à la face verdâtre d'un noyé; le dessin grimaçant convulsionnait les traits, rendant ainsi la sinistre ressemblance plus frappante' (pp.68-69). Camille's decomposing corpse in the Morgue is described in much the same terms: 'Camille était ignoble. (...) Sa face paraissait encore ferme et rigide; les traits s'étaient conservés, la peau avait seulement pris une teinte jaunâtre et boueuse. La tête, maigre, osseuse, légèrement tuméfiée, grimaçait' (p.129).

Zola exploits this dovetailing of art and reality to produce a moment of terror for a panic-stricken Laurent, when the murderer mistakes the portrait for Camille himself: 'il vit Camille dans un coin plein d'ombre (...). La face de sa victime était verdâtre et convulsionnée, telle qu'il l'avait aperçue sur une dalle de la Morgue' (p.194). The shocked state of the breathless Laurent, 'dont les cheveux se dressaient' (p.194), is relayed through an emotionally-charged lexis, in which nouns such as *trouble* and *effroi* are complemented by the equally powerful verbs *épouvanter*, *étonner*, and *écraser* (pp.194-95). There is no relief from his victim's accusatory stare: 'Mais le portrait eut un regard si écrasant, si ignoble, si long, que Laurent, après avoir voulu lutter de fixité avec lui, fut vaincu et recula' (p.195). The morbid pruriency Laurent attributes to his victim reveals the darker side of his sexual guilt: 'La pensée que Camille était là, dans un coin, le guettant, assistant à sa nuit de noces, les examinant, Thérèse et lui, acheva de rendre Laurent fou de terreur et de désespoir' (p.196).

Camille reappears in a multiplicity of guises whenever Laurent attempts a new canvas. The murderer sees only too well how his guilt has been exteriorized in his artistic endeavours: 'Laurent comprit qu'il avait trop regardé Camille à la Morgue. L'image du cadavre s'était gravée profondément en lui. Maintenant, sa main, sans qu'il en eût conscience, traçait toujours les lignes de ce visage atroce dont le souvenir le suivait partout' (p.231). As each painting confirms the power of the dead over the living, Laurent has the decidedly uncomfortable feeling that he has been possessed by his victim: 'Cette pensée que ses doigts avaient la faculté fatale et inconsciente de reproduire sans cesse le portrait de Camille lui fit regarder sa main avec terreur. Il lui semblait que cette main ne lui appartenait plus' (p.232).

The scar

For Laurent, the undeniable presence of Camille is also found in the flesh-wound inflicted by his desperate victim. The resultant scar brands Laurent as a criminal, and becomes the concrete manifestation of his uneasy conscience.

The pain Laurent experiences is expressed in terms of traditional tortures: 'La morsure de Camille était comme un fer rouge posé sur sa peau (...). Il lui semblait qu'une douzaine d'aiguilles pénétraient peu à peu dans sa chair' (p.123). The ugly wound reflects the vile crime: 'Cette plaie faisait un trou rouge, large comme une pièce de deux sous; la peau avait été arrachée, la chair se montrait, rosâtre, avec des taches noires; des filets de sang avaient coulé jusqu'à l'épaule, en minces traînées qui s'écaillaient' (p.123). During his separation from Thérèse, the scar, as though dormant, does not trouble him, but once his marriage has been arranged, the scar responds aggressively: 'il sentit sous ses doigts la cicatrice de la morsure de Camille. (...) Il fut terrifié en la retrouvant sur sa peau, il crut qu'elle lui mangeait la chair. (...) et il la·sentit toujours, dévorante, trouant son cou' (p.153). Zola records the curious behaviour of the tumescent scar: 'La cicatrice fut empourprée par le flot qui montait, elle devint vive et sanglante, elle se détacha, toute rouge, sur le cou gras et blanc. En même temps, Laurent ressentit des picotements aigus, comme si l'on eût enfoncé des aiguilles dans la plaie' (p.157).

Whenever Laurent seeks to profit from his crime, the scar asserts itself. As he dresses for the wedding ceremony he receives an untimely reminder of his victim: 'il aperçut la morsure de Camille toute rouge; le faux col avait légèrement écorché la cicatrice' (p.180). Imagination fuels his guilty conscience: 'à toutes les minutes de cette longue journée, il avait senti les dents du noyé qui lui entraient dans la peau. Il s'imaginait par moments qu'un filet de sang lui coulait sur la poitrine et allait tacher de rouge la blancheur de son gilet' (p.183). Maddened by the irritation, he brutally forces Thérèse to kiss the wound, convinced that this will end the pain and rid him of Camille's memory (p.193). Thérèse eventually responds willingly, even sadistically: 'elle éprouvait une volupté âcre à poser sa bouche sur cette peau où s'étaient enfoncées les dents de Camille. Un instant, elle eut la pensée de mordre son mari à cet endroit, d'arracher un large morceau de chair, de faire une nouvelle blessure, plus profonde, qui emporterait les marques de l'ancienne' (pp.210-11).

As the action draws to its close, Zola, in the tradition of the Gothic tale, underlines the moral significance of Laurent's scar and offers the horrific image of a degenerate character entirely covered in scar-tissue:

> Sa souffrance la plus aiguë, souffrance physique et morale, lui venait de la morsure que Camille lui avait faite au cou. A certain moments, il s'imaginait que cette cicatrice lui couvrait tout le corps. (...) Cette sorte de blessure vivant sur lui, se réveillant, rougissant et le mordant au moindre trouble, l'effrayait et le torturait. (...) Il portait ainsi partout avec lui le souvenir vivant et dévorant de son crime. (p.280)

In the melodramatic final scene of the double suicide, the scar, again foregrounded, links Thérèse and Laurent with Camille in death: 'La bouche de la jeune femme alla heurter, sur le cou de son mari, la cicatrice qu'avaient laissée les dents de Camille' (p.301).

The cat

Further manifestations of the adulterous couple's guilt-feelings are found in the presence of the household cat, François. For Robert Lethbridge, he functions 'as the psychological correlative of the protagonists' (*31*, p.292). From the outset, the cat is party to the lovers' meetings, and he serves to exteriorize their troubled conscience. They fantasize that he is Camille's spy and will pass on details of their affair (p.79). Laurent finds the cat's appearance unnerving: 'ses yeux seuls paraissaient vivants; et il y avait, dans les coins de sa gueule, deux plis profonds qui faisaient éclater de rire cette tête d'animal empaillé' (p.80). Later, in the grip of fear, the murderer imagines that the cat has an avenging role: 'Dans cette heure de fièvre et de crainte, il crut que le chat allait lui sauter au visage pour venger Camille. Cette bête devait tout savoir' (p.196). His obsession persuades him that Camille's spirit has entered the cat, and that François will speak with his voice (p.197). The cat's unwavering eyes, now with an unnerving 'éclat métallique' (p.197), anticipate the steely stare of the paralysed Mme Raquin, whose eyes 'étaient devenus noirs et durs, pareils à des morceaux de métal' (p.240). The increasingly disturbed Laurent readily makes the connection: 'le meurtrier de Camille établissait une vague ressemblance entre cette bête irritée et la paralytique. Il se disait que le chat, ainsi que Mme Raquin, connaissait le crime et le dénoncerait, si jamais il parlait un jour' (p.282). Laurent's killing of François is needlessly violent, and the painful death of the murderer's second victim is recounted in distressing detail: 'Pendant toute la nuit, la misérable bête se traîna le long de la gouttière, l'échine brisée, en poussant des miaulements rauques' (p.282). The full horror of Laurent's demented act is registered in the distraught reactions of the two female observers: 'Mme Raquin pleura François presque autant qu'elle avait pleuré Camille; Thérèse eut une atroce crise de nerfs' (p.282).

Zola's aspirations to the realist scientific mode might temper, but could never entirely control, the dark shaping forces of his melodramatic vision. In the final analysis, the compelling attraction of his tale of adultery and murder depends rather less on the framework of spurious science, than on the rhetorical elements the narrative shares with the traditions of the Gothic novel.

6. Theatre

'J'estime qu'il est toujours dangereux de tirer un drame d'un roman' (Zola, Preface to his play *Thérèse Raquin*, 25 July 1873)

During the 1860s Zola's involvement with the theatre, both as drama critic and aspiring playwright, provided a formative testing-ground for his literary principles. In his play reviews and commentaries on contemporary theatrical practice, he advocated a naturalist approach consistent with his views on the novel, though as the author of only unperformed plays he was as yet unable to offer a practical demonstration of his theories. In 1867 there came valuable experience of adaptation for the stage when, with Marius Roux, he extensively reworked his novel *Les Mystères de Marseille* to create a melodrama of the same title. In the following year, he complemented this experience by turning his rejected play *Madeleine* into the novel *Madeleine Férat* (1868). After further periods as drama critic, most notably for *Le Globe* and for *L'Avenir national*, Zola undertook the adaptation of *Thérèse Raquin*, and theory finally became practice when the play opened on 11 July 1873 at the Théâtre de la Renaissance. As a working demonstration of naturalist concepts refined over almost a decade of drama reviews, Zola's stage version of *Thérèse Raquin* is of considerable interest.

From his first articles, Zola had urged radical reforms. The bland clichés of boulevard theatre together with the diverting stagecraft of the well-made play were rejected in favour of naturalist experimentation: 'Il s'agit nettement de savoir ce que deviendra notre théâtre, si l'on pourra appliquer à la scène cet amour d'analyse et de psychologie qui nous donne en ce moment une génération nouvelle de romanciers' (*21*, 10, p.117). He cites *Le Drame de la rue de la*

Paix by Adolphe Belot as a play which met his criteria: 'je crois y avoir trouvé autre chose que de la science dramatique; il m'a semblé y sentir passer un peu de ce souffle d'analyse physiologique et psychologique qui féconde en ce moment le roman et l'histoire' (*21*, 10, p.1048). Zola's comments have particular significance because of his association with the author who had, in part, inspired *Thérèse Raquin*. During the summer of 1868 the two writers appear to have been engaged in a collaborative venture. In a letter to Zola dated 16 June 1868, Belot alludes to their joint undertaking: 'Je pense à votre pièce. (...) Nous bâtirons le plan du drame en quelques heures' (*20*, 2, p.119 note 4). This may well have been the first projected, though unrealized, adaptation of *Thérèse Raquin*.

Henri Mitterand (*32*) argues that Zola probably began work on the eventual adaptation at the end of 1872 or the beginning of 1873. Zola's correspondence, however, points to an earlier period, with a first draft of the play possibly in existence by the spring of 1872. In a letter dated 13 February 1872, he reveals his trepidation at writing for the stage: 'Avez-vous remarqué la chute fatale des romanciers au théâtre? (...) Cela m'effraie un peu pour moi' (*20*, 2, pp.314-15). Letters between Zola and Belot during 1872 chart protracted negotiations with M. Billion, director of the Ambigu theatre, to stage *Thérèse Raquin* in the winter season of that year. On 2 May 1872, Zola reported: 'J'ai vu hier M. Billion que j'ai trouvé d'abord très effrayé par *Thérèse Raquin*. Sans le rassurer complètement, je suis parvenu à obtenir de lui la promesse qu'il tenterait sans doute la représentation de mon drame, l'hiver prochain' (*20*, 2, p.316). That promise, however, was not kept. In February 1873, Zola resumed his role as theatre critic, now for *L'Avenir national*.

His dramatic criteria remained resolutely the same. Real life situations are preferred: 'Notre théâtre doit être (...) une étude réelle de la vie' (*21*, 10, p.1071). Flesh and blood characters are essential: 'Il faut créer des hommes, avant tout, au théâtre comme ailleurs. Les situations ne sont plus ensuite que les actes mêmes des personnages, les résultantes de leurs caractères' (*21*, 10, p.1077). Powerful drama is achieved by a clinical demonstration of human behaviour: 'Le cadavre humain, la bête humaine, est étalée sur la pierre d'amphithéâtre. En trois coups de scalpel, les chairs sont à nu, et la démonstration est faite. Là, est le théâtre moderne, selon moi, dans cette littérature expérimentale' (*21*, 10, p.1100). In effect, Zola was preparing the ground for his adaptation of *Thérèse Raquin*.

In his Preface to the published play, dated 25 July 1875, Zola alludes to Ulbach's taunt in 'La Littérature putride', that naturalist novels could not make good drama: 'des critiques (...) m'avaient formellement mis au défi d'en tirer un drame (...). Il y avait provocation' (*21*, 15, p.121). He explains his approach to meet this challenge. To achieve a faithful transposition of the determinist concept he had concentrated the action in a single location: 'Alors j'ai suivi le roman pas à pas; j'ai enfermé le drame dans la même chambre, humide et noire, afin de ne rien lui ôter de son relief, ni de sa fatalité' (ibid., p.123). The pressures and frustrations of everyday life were reflected through character and situation, with an emphasis on the natural rather than the theatrical: 'j'ai choisi des comparses sots et inutiles, pour mettre, sous les angoisses atroces de mes héros, la banalité de la vie de tous les jours; j'ai tenté de ramener continuellement la mise en scène aux occupations ordinaires de mes personnages, de façon à ce qu'ils ne "jouent" pas, mais à ce qu'ils "vivent" devant le public' (ibid., p.123).

The action of Zola's play is divided into four acts, and is confined to the Raquin apartment. The original theatre programme had indicated a scene at Saint-Ouen depicting the murder, but this was suppressed before the first performance, thus maintaining the unity of place. The original characters are retained with the exception of Olivier; Suzanne, his wife in the novel, becomes Michaud's unmarried niece. The dramatic development is essentially that of the novel.

The play opens with Laurent completing Camille's portrait, and by the close of the first act all the characters have been introduced, the adultery revealed, and the murder planned. These details occupy Chapters I-XII of the novel. The second act is concerned with the repercussions of Camille's supposedly accidental drowning, and the promotion of Thérèse's remarriage to Laurent (XIII-XIX). The third act opens after the ceremony, with the unhappy couple unable to rekindle their passion, and sharing their horrific memories of the crime. Mme Raquin, overhearing their confessions, suffers total paralysis (XX-XXV). In the final act, Mme Raquin fails to unmask the criminals, but in the last scene she suddenly regains her powers of speech to pass judgement on them. As she gloats over their double suicide, vengeance is hers (XXVI-XXXII).

A comparison between the novel and Zola's treatment for the stage reveals both the immediate differences and the problems posed by adapting the naturalist text.

Zola condensed and concentrated the action and, in doing so, omitted the developmental stages of crucial events. Thus, the exposition of Thérèse's cumulative frustrations which lead to her adultery is sacrificed, as is the account of the pressures resulting in Camille's murder. Similarly, Mme Raquin's gradual deterioration is simplified to a sudden paralysis when she realizes that Camille's death was not an accident. The novel's third-person narrator, while introducing both characters and situations naturally and economically, had created temporal perspectives through the summary mode. Zola's adaptation relies on the intervals between the four acts to mark the passage of time and to cover key events, so that the murder is deemed to have taken place between Act 1 and Act 2, and the marriage between Act 2 and Act 3. Consequently, at the start of each act, characters are required to recall, somewhat artificially, the intervening events.

As Henri Mitterand (*32*) notes, rhetoric has replaced analysis. Zola relies heavily on those chapters already rich in dialogue, to the exclusion of those in which description or analysis is found. Laurent's nightmares and hallucinations, for example, so convincingly related in Chapters XVII-XVIII, have no stage equivalent. There is similarly no place for Thérèse's horrific imaginings concerning her pregnancy, nor for her final debauchery.

Zola seeks to convey his formative environments and atmospheric settings through a detailed *mise en scène*. In the final act, for example, the psychological deterioration of the protagonists is suggested through the neglected apartment: 'Rideaux sales.

Ménage abandonné, poussière, torchons oubliés sur les sièges, vaisselle traînant sur les meubles' (*21*, 15, p.184). As Janice Best (*11*) has pointed out, objects too become visual metaphors, so that the murdered Camille's empty chair comes to denote his invisible presence.

With the exception of Mme Raquin and Suzanne, the main roles show little change. Suzanne achieves greater prominence with an episodic fairy-tale romance which serves to point up the bleak reality of Thérèse's situation. Mme Raquin's role is also transformed when, in the final scene, she suddenly recovers her speech to condemn the guilty couple.[5] This last-minute intervention increases the melodrama already inherent in Zola's original conception.

Staged at the close of the Parisian theatrical season, the play ran for only nine performances, but nevertheless merited serious reviews.[6] As well as several revivals, there have been new adaptations. These later versions confirm the enduring attraction of Zola's narrative, and provide illuminating points of comparison.

The Marcelle Maurette version

In June 1947, an adaptation of Zola's novel by Mme Marcelle Maurette (*8*) received its first performance by the Marie Bell company during its tour of South America. The following year, with the celebrated actress again in the role of Thérèse, the play opened in Paris at the Théâtre du Gymnase on 12 April, and ran for sixty performances before closing on 17 May.

The play is divided into three acts and twelve tableaux. The action takes place in, and around, the Raquin shop in Second Empire Paris and, although there are some shifts of emphasis, the dramatic development is largely faithful to Zola's original conception. The

---

[5] According to Paul Alexis, this speech was included to placate the actress Marie Laurent who would have preferred the role of Thérèse. See: *Emile Zola. Notes d'un ami*, Paris, Charpentier, 1882, pp.133-34.
[6] For a detailed account of the play's critical reception and the history of its performances, see Henri Mitterand (*32*, pp.504-16).

novel's characters are retained with the exception of Olivier and Suzanne, while a new character, a prostitute, is introduced.

The first four tableaux of Act 1 establish the main characters and Thérèse's frustrations. The fifth tableau reveals Thérèse and Laurent as lovers, with Thérèse recounting her unhappy upbringing and loveless marriage. After narrowly avoiding discovery by Mme Raquin, the couple resolve to arrange a future without Camille. A boating trip is planned.

The second act opens with the wedding celebrations of Thérèse and Laurent, and recollections of Laurent's heroism in vainly trying to save the drowned Camille. Left alone, the couple find that passion has deserted them. Thérèse fears that Camille will haunt them, and Laurent tells of his nightmares. Mme Raquin's paralysis is reported. In a rapidly-deteriorating relationship, Laurent extorts money from Thérèse to rent an artist's studio by tormenting her with details of Camille's murder. A distressed Mme Raquin overhears this account of events.

The final act opens with Laurent inviting a prostitute to share the marital bed as revenge for Thérèse's apparent infidelities. At the Thursday gathering, Michaud recalls a couple who committed suicide after being haunted by their victim's ghost. Mme Raquin vainly tries to denounce the murderers who, after disputing responsibility for the crime, take their own lives.

As with Zola's own adaptation, the Maurette version loses the novel's detailed exposition of characterical motivation, as the action moves rapidly from one dramatic event to another. The intervals between the tableaux or the acts are again used to collapse time. This is most evident between Act 1 and Act 2, when not only has Camille met his death, but his murderers have also celebrated their marriage. The novel's atmospheric descriptions are replaced by stage sets designed to represent the mental states of the characters, and by lighting effects, now watery-green, now blood-red, which serve only to emphasize the intrinsic melodrama of the action.

Zola's powerful evocations of Laurent's nightmares are lost, and the anguish suffered by Thérèse and Laurent is replaced, in a pale transposition, by Michaud's story of the haunting. With the omission of Camille's portrait, an important aspect of the victim's imagined presence is lost, though there are attempts to suggest his unwanted company with wind billowing in the curtains, and references to the cat. A superficial illusion of fidelity to Zola is generated by the use of dialogue taken directly from the novel.

Once again the main characters have undergone only minor modification. Mme Raquin, for example, is older and already infirm at the outset, and has a less powerful presence. On the other hand, Grivet and Michaud enjoy more developed roles as comic, invariably squabbling, companions, who counterpoint the misery of Thérèse and Laurent as the haunted couple. The unhappy pair are presented sympathetically as star-crossed lovers driven to desperate solutions. Camille remains a pathetic creature, but is endowed with more self-awareness than in Zola's portrayal. The additional character, the prostitute, is derived from Zola's account of Laurent's debauchery in the novel's penultimate chapter. This episode has no place in the author's own adaptation.

The Raymond Rouleau version

For the 1981-82 season at the Théâtre de Boulogne-Billancourt, Raymond Rouleau (9) staged his own adaptation of *Thérèse Raquin*. The play enjoyed an acclaimed first run from 2 October to 8 November 1981, and was performed again as part of the same season between 12 and 31 January 1982.

The action is recounted through five tableaux, and takes place in three principal locations: the Raquin household, Laurent's studio, and the banks of the Seine at Vernon. The cast of characters includes a group of canoeists, but omits Olivier.

The play opens at the Raquin household with Laurent putting the finishing touches to Camille's portrait. Left alone, Thérèse and Laurent embrace. The other characters are introduced. Suzanne has no tears for her dead father, who had raped and abused her. In a monologue, Camille recognizes the failure of his marriage. The second tableau finds Thérèse at Laurent's studio. She is pregnant by him, cannot face returning to Camille, and looks to her lover for a solution.

The third tableau transposes the action to the Seine at Vernon. Thérèse and Laurent leave a dozing Camille for an emotionally-charged discussion about their future. Left alone, Camille articulates his strong attachment to Laurent. The latter, now determined to get rid of the unwanted husband, returns to the river-bank. After a struggle in which Camille bites him on the neck, Laurent drowns his rival in the river. Passing canoeists corroborate Laurent's story that he had been trying to rescue the unfortunate Camille. A shocked Thérèse has a miscarriage.

The action of the fourth tableau is set some eight months later. The tragic 'accident' is recalled. Camille's body is still missing. Persuaded by Michaud, an ailing Mme Raquin agrees to Thérèse becoming Laurent's wife, though both partners appear diffident.

The final tableau opens with the marriage celebrations. Later, in the bedroom, Thérèse senses Camille's presence in the cat. A frustrated Laurent tries to force a reluctant Thérèse to consummate the marriage. In his anger he destroys Camille's portrait with its seemingly accusing stare. Mme Raquin, overhearing the couple's revelations about Camille's death, is struck dumb. Her subsequent efforts to unmask the guilty couple come to nothing. The final scene pictures a debauched Thérèse, now dressed as a prostitute, and a broken Laurent regretting both his involvement with Thérèse and the murder of Camille. For her part, Thérèse acknowledges that Laurent killed for love. With Mme Raquin as a silent witness, the distraught couple commit suicide.

Although Rouleau has reworked a number of details, he still captures much of the raw strength of Zola's narrative. With the exception of the Morgue, he reproduces the novel's principal locations, and places on stage the key dramatic moments, including the murder. Present too, are several elements the previous adaptations either played down or failed to retain: the role of Camille's portrait, Laurent's neck wound, the canoeists' evidence, the presence of the cat and Thérèse's debauchery. The main characters and their

situations are established economically, and the pressures leading to
Camille's murder are made apparent.

In Rouleau's version, the violence of the characters' emotions
comes through, both in their conduct and in their language. The
action is occasionally quite physical. Thérèse, far from being a
sultry, depressed individual is, from the outset, a lively presence.
During the horseplay with Laurent and Camille in the first tableau
she addresses them in turn as *lavette, couille molle*, and *cul terreux*
(*9*, p.8). Her affair with Laurent is convincingly passionate, and her
pregnancy brings an additional realistic pressure. Laurent is suitably
physical in his dealings, not only with Thérèse and Camille, but also
with Mme Raquin whom he seems prepared to kill. Thérèse and
Laurent appear as a couple dominated by passion, and fatally trapped
by circumstances.

Camille, as an asthmatic given to self-irony and with passive
homosexual leanings towards Laurent, is a much more rounded
character than in previous stage versions. His monologues, in which
he recognizes his inadequacies and admits to his loveless marriage,
bring a new dimension to the role. His pathetic openness is matched
by the frankness of Suzanne, now presented as the victim of her
father's incestuous passions. Her down-to-earth view of people and
events serves to reinforce the bleaker mood of the play. In this
respect, her role differs from that of Zola's character, whose naïve
fantasies were used contrastively to highlight the painful reality of
Thérèse's situation.

The general conception of Rouleau's play, with its raw
emotions, frank sexual discussions, powerfully-drawn personalities
and realistically-depicted locations, is very much in the spirit of
Zola's intentions. For the critic Jean Vigneron (*36*), Rouleau's
adaptation was 'un modèle de respect du roman original,
d'intelligente transposition scénique et de spectacle exigeant et
précis. Zola lui-même, auteur de la première adaptation de son livre,
n'y aurait sans doute rien trouvé à redire.'

As Zola recognized, adapting *Thérèse Raquin* for the stage had
been a calculated risk with only limited success. That later play-
wrights have been tempted to create their own versions of his

powerful story points to a recognition of the intrinsic dramatic potential in his original conception. The twentieth century has witnessed not only new stagings of Zola's play, but also successive adaptations, and, with the advent of the cinema, yet further opportunities arose to bring Zola's work in a fresh form to an even larger public.

7. Cinema

'Zola voyait *ciné*' (Henry de Forge,
'Discours au pèlerinage de Medan',
2 October 1932)

Since the earliest days of the cinema, Zola's fiction has been an attractive source of screenplays for the film-maker. As early as 1902, Ferdinand Zecca had made a film based on *L'Assommoir*, and before the end of the decade both *Germinal* and *Nana* were also to pass before the cameras. Over the intervening years, the majority of Zola's novels have been brought to the screen and, in many instances, more than once, by successive generations of film directors. *Thérèse Raquin* has proved to be no exception.

The first of three silent films, all now sadly lost, was made in 1911 by the Danish director Einar Zangenberg. Four years later, a version by the Italian director Nino Martoglio, which respected Zola's Second Empire period and reproduced locations in meticulous detail, came to have a seminal influence on the development of neo-realist film aesthetics. Finally, in 1928, there appeared one of the triumphs of the silent period, the version by Jacques Feyder.

The director's Franco-German co-production boasted stars from both countries: Gina Manès as Thérèse, Wolfgang Zilzer as Camille, Hans-Adalbert von Schlettow as Laurent and, as Mme Raquin, Jeanne-Marie Laurent, the grand-daughter of Marie Laurent who had created the role for the stage. Although the film's contemporary setting with its motor cars attracted a degree of criticism, Feyder's three-hour-long adaptation remained remarkably faithful to Zola's narrative. With the major exception of the Morgue episode, the original structure is respected, and in its discreet handling of scenes such as the murder and the aftermath, here represented by ever-widening ripples of water, the film was considered by some to be a distinct improvement on the explicitness of the original.

In 1953, Marcel Carné, who had been an assistant to Feyder, directed the first sound version of *Thérèse Raquin*, based on a script written in collaboration with Charles Spaak. The cast of French and Italian actors reflected the requirements of the Franco-Italian co-production, and the strong team included Sylvie as Mme Raquin, Simone Signoret as Thérèse, Jacques Duby as Camille, and the contemporary Italian star, Raf Vallone, as Laurent. Of Zola's minor figures, only Grivet and Michaud were retained. Two characters were added: Riton, a demobbed sailor, played by Roland Lesaffre, and Georgette, a hotel maid, played by Anna-Maria Casilio. Both Simone Signoret and Roland Lesaffre received awards for their performances, and, at the Venice Film Festival, the film shared the supreme award with Fellini's *La Strada*.

For a director like Carné, renowned for fatalistic romantic melodramas such as *Quai des brumes* and *Le Jour se lève*, Zola's novel would appear perfect film material. However, whereas his pre-war films were conceived in collaboration with Jacques Prévert, *Thérèse Raquin* was scripted by Charles Spaak and, as Carné himself recognized, the sentimental pessimism of the late thirties had given way to the more cynical spirit of the fifties. Although his creative impulses remained firmly rooted in the poetic realism of the earlier period, Carné's version of *Thérèse Raquin* reflects changing social circumstances and public attitudes. Aware that it would be unwise simply to attempt a re-make of the Feyder version he so greatly admired, Carné opted for a modernized reworking of Zola's text. The novel is freely adapted, with the updated action set in Lyons in the nineteen-fifties.

Carné argued that his changes were essential:

> pour actualiser l'intrigue, il fallait opérer de sérieux remaniements: dans le développement même du récit. Pas une fois, dans l'ouvrage, il n'est question de divorce: une seule issue pour les amants: tuer le mari. Nous avons dû pour être logiques et tenir compte de l'évolution des

> moeurs, envisager d'autres solutions. Le crime n'a plus
> alors nécessairement son caractère de préméditation; il
> se produit une série de circonstances: mais, comme dans
> le livre, brusquement nos deux héros se trouvent devant
> l'horreur d'un forfait qui les sépare... (*15*, pp.64-65)

With the memory that Feyder's faithfully-reproduced haunting of
Thérèse and Laurent had been considered the film's weakness, Carné
decided on a fundamental change to Zola's conception. The couple's
anguish and punishment would no longer come in the form of a
guilty conscience and its exteriorized manifestations, but through
external human agencies, and principally through a blackmailing
sailor:

> il fallait, pour maintenir l'intérêt du spectateur moderne,
> trouver autre chose que le drame du remords. Nous
> avons été amenés à imaginer un rebondissement en
> créant un personnage nouveau, celui du témoin qui va
> tenter de tirer parti de l'affaire en soutirant de l'argent
> aux coupables. Le ton naturaliste du début change alors.
> Ce personnage, pour nous, c'est le Destin qui, de
> nouveau, réunit les amants et, finalement, les perd à
> jamais... (ibid., p.65)

As Carné indicates, his film narrative follows the tone and pattern of
the first part of Zola's story, incorporating many of the initial situations and characterial elements, albeit in transposed forms. It is in
the second part, with the introduction of the blackmailer, that the
most fundamental divergence is to be observed.

After three economical establishing shots of Lyons, the camera
takes the audience to a game of riverside *boules*. Camille and Mme
Raquin watch enthralled, while Thérèse gazes listlessly at the Rhône.
Mme Raquin, a pampering and possessive mother, is openly hostile
towards her daughter-in-law, Thérèse, trapped in her joyless
marriage to the sickly Camille. While the two women run the
draper's shop, Camille works as a junior customs clerk. One day he

strikes up a friendship with Laurent, a well-built, outgoing, but quick-tempered, Italian lorry-driver. Laurent returns a drunk and sentimental Camille to the shop and, delighted to discover Thérèse, he readily accepts an invitation to Mme Raquin's Thursday gatherings. The ritual board games, which dominate these evenings, hold little appeal for either Thérèse or Laurent.

Laurent declares his love for Thérèse, and pleads with her to leave Camille, but Thérèse feels duty-bound to stay with her husband. One evening, while the others are absorbed in their fatuous game, the couple become lovers. They contrive a meeting in the café of a local park and, at Thérèse's suggestion, Laurent comes to the apartment above the shop. The couple only narrowly escape detection by Mme Raquin, and Laurent resolves to bring the affair into the open.

Camille resorts to emotional blackmail to keep Thérèse, but without success. She does, however, agree to go to Paris with him to discuss their situation, little knowing that Camille intends to incarcerate her with a relative. Thérèse tells Laurent of the planned journey. Alarmed at this unforeseen development, Laurent succeeds in joining the Paris train at Mâcon. A heated quarrel ensues between the two men and, during a struggle in the corridor, Camille falls from the train. No-one appears to have witnessed these events, and the lovers quickly devise a plan to avoid implication in Camille's death. Laurent leaves the train at the next station and Thérèse, when questioned by the police, claims to have been asleep during Camille's disappearance. A fellow-passenger, a demobbed sailor, corroborates this story. However, when Thérèse identifies the body, the police make it clear that they are far from satisfied that Camille fell accidentally to his death. Thérèse suspects that Mme Raquin, now paralysed by shock, knows the truth, and the lovers agree to a temporary separation. The sailor, reading a newspaper account of Camille's death, recognizes an opportunity for blackmail.

At Laurent's insistence, the guilty couple eventually meet, but only to dispute responsibility for the crime. Thérèse, still deeply affected by events, ends the affair, and remains unresponsive to Laurent's telephone calls. Alone with Mme Raquin, Thérèse sentimentalizes her life with Camille, and aggressively rejects the public rumours surrounding the circumstances of his death.

The sailor arrives to extort money. His action precipitates renewed contact between Thérèse and Laurent, and the couple decide to run away. However, the sailor thwarts their escape and, after a violent altercation with Laurent, sets a deadline for payment. Meanwhile, a verdict of accidental death is returned on Camille, and Thérèse receives opportune financial compensation for his loss. The money will serve to buy off the blackmailer, who has instructed an innocent hotel maid to post a letter incriminating Thérèse and Laurent, should he fail to return from his meeting with them. Thérèse and Laurent hand over the money, and at last feel secure. However, outside the shop, the blackmailer is killed by a runaway lorry, and the letter, sealing the fate of Thérèse and Laurent, is duly posted.

As the full extent of Carné's reworking becomes apparent, many readers will judge the film to be an unacceptable betrayal of the author's purpose. Those expecting a detailed transcription of Zola's Second Empire settings, and protagonists haunted, and ultimately destroyed, by memories of their crime, will be disappointed. The novel's pattern is rejected in favour of a theoretically more plausible narrative logic. Zola's determinism, his inner physiologically-based forces of retribution, is replaced by Carné's conception of fate, whose principal agent is the blackmailer. This change marks the most significant departure from the author's stoutly defended pseudo-scientific thesis. Indeed, in terms of its modernized detail, narrative structures, and value-system, Carné's film poses a challenge to certain conceptions of screen adaptation.

On the premise that a film version should reproduce as faithfully as possible the essence of the original literary construct, discussion necessarily focuses on differences and similarities. In this respect, the updated action and changed locations of Carné's version must be counted as transgressions. Even setting aside for a moment the presence of the blackmailing sailor, Zola's original characters have undergone modifications, and the degree to which they have survived transposition to the twentieth-century medium must be considered further.

Originally conceived as demonstrations of nineteenth-century determinist theories, Zola's creations are now refracted inconsistently and imperfectly through the optic of twentieth-century existentialist assumptions about individual freedom, self-determination and bourgeois morality.

Thérèse, idly watching the Rhône flow by, or dreamily observing lovers in the street, remains the bored and unfulfilled wife of the feeble Camille. She refuses freedom with Laurent and, citing her debt to Mme Raquin who raised her, condemns herself to be a prisoner of her past. Less passionate and more rational than Zola's Thérèse, Carné's heroine is seen to act decisively after the murder. It is she who is required to identify the body and to deal initially with the blackmailer. Though recognizing her crime, she is not consumed by feelings of remorse. Her punishment, when it comes, seems to be no more than bad luck.

Camille, her self-centred, inadequate and mother-dominated husband, is instantly recognizable from the novel. He is pitifully officious at work, and in turn both devious and manipulative with his wife and friends. He cheats at games and secretly plans to lock Thérèse away. He will turn on Laurent as a foreigner, and self-righteously invoke his legal rights in an attempt to deny Thérèse her freedom. His role, unlike that of Zola's character, ceases with his death.

Laurent, the virile, pragmatic sensualist of Zola's text, is no longer a minor clerk with artistic aspirations, but a plain-speaking, self-employed Italian lorry driver. He is a free individual with no roots and no constraints. His feelings for Thérèse rise above the brutal passions which motivated Zola's character. However, like his literary counterpart, he is the antithesis of his rival Camille: he is strong, handsome, outgoing and lively. The two men are contrasted when the powerful Laurent carries the lightweight Camille into the shop. Laurent's energy is matched by a quick temper, and he responds spontaneously to provocation. Thus the death of Camille is not premeditated: Laurent simply reacts characteristically to

Camille's verbal abuse. He experiences no sense of guilt after the murder.

In the film's reshaped narrative, Mme Raquin's role is greatly reduced. She is still the doting mother whose son must win at games but, in her open hostility towards Thérèse, she appears even more unattractive. Her paralysed presence after the murder becomes largely gratuitous, since she is no longer the instrument of retribution and does not attempt to reveal the culprits. In many respects, her role has been subsumed into that of the blackmailer.

As the instrument, but also the victim of fate, the blackmailer replaces the forces of Zola's physiological determinism. His reminiscences of his harsh upbringing and of his recent war service establish his credentials as a self-sufficient character.[7] Refusing the label of blackmailer, he considers himself a fundamentally decent individual. He acts correctly with the hotel maid and, in his death-throes, vainly attempts to reverse the fatal mechanism he has devised.

Though producing insights into the workings both of the original text and the secondary film version, such comparative, quantitative approaches may be considered ultimately of limited value in promoting an appreciation of the film as a work in its own right. As George Bluestone has observed, 'changes are *inevitable* the moment one abandons the linguistic for the visual medium' (*12*, p.15). The point is well made that each art form is autonomous, and is therefore most productively discussed in terms of its own specificities. In this perspective, the film-maker is released from the slavish role of merely providing an illustrated version of the literary text, to create in its place a work reflecting his own particular reading, and determined by his own individual film practice. As Bela Balázs has contended, the film-maker 'may use the existing work of art merely as raw material, regard it from the specific angle of his own art form as if it were raw reality, and pay no attention to the form once already given to the material' (*10*, p.263).

For several film critics, Carné's *Thérèse Raquin* does succeed as a cinematic expression of its literary antecedent, in spirit if not in

---

[7] The role was partly inspired by Roland Lesaffre's war service in the Pacific. See Marcel Carné (*13*, p.328.)

detail. Jacques Doniol-Valcroze commented, 'on s'aperçoit que malgré tout Carné et Spaak ont été assez fidèles à Zola, sinon dans la lettre du moins dans l'esprit' (*24*, p.42). Jean Dutourd (*27*) concurred: 'on y a ajouté et retranché. Et pourtant, il est indiscutable que l'esprit de Zola règne dans l'oeuvre d'un bout à l'autre... Il [le film] traduit le roman à sa façon, une façon cinématographique, dramatique. Il nous donne une version possible de *Thérèse Raquin*.' An even more enthusiastic François Vinneuil (*37*) contended that Carné's adaptation represented a triumph for cinema over literature: 'Le problème de l'adaptation littéraire est résolu, cette fois, par l'éclatante supériorité, en richesse humaine, en vigueur artistique, de l'oeuvre cinématographique sur le roman.' These claims may be tested by focusing attention on the film-maker's means of presentation.

Carné's direction is generally unemphatic and unobtrusive. There is no attempt to reproduce Zola's commentaries, or his foregrounding of characters, by an omniscient voice-over narration, though a non-verbal rhetoric is derived from the film's *mise en scène*, sound-track and camera-work. In the first half of his updated version, Carné respects Zola's basic narrative elements by substituting modern equivalents, and reflects the novel's atmosphere through a carefully-executed *mise en scène*.

After his economical introduction to Lyons, Carné takes the action to the oppressive Raquin apartment with its cluttered, old-fashioned rooms, its windows heavily-curtained and shuttered, and its doors kept firmly closed. The claustrophobic atmosphere reflects Mme Raquin's overprotective influence, while Thérèse's wistful appearance at the window suggests her feeling of entrapment. The sense of constriction produced by these heavy, and often gloomy, interiors is reinforced by the high walls of the narrow streets. These elements provide an effective contrast to the sunlit open spaces of the park and the brightly-lit café, where Thérèse and Laurent find freedom. Whereas Camille, Mme Raquin and her guests seem an integral part of the dreary apartment, Laurent's natural habitat lies in more public places, and Thérèse, released from the family prison, blossoms in his company.

For Carné, a character's appearance is conceived as an important visual signal for the audience. The feeble Camille is immediately identified with scarves, hats and overcoats, whereas the vital Laurent sports a black leather jacket and casual sweaters. Thérèse, in Camille's company, wears dark clothes with her hair pinned back, but with Laurent she puts on a white blouse and, with her hair let down, looks both happy and younger.

The screen space accorded to individuals may denote either the relationship between them or serve, as an objective correlative, to indicate their particular situation. Thus, the opening sequence shows the closeness of Camille and his mother, as together they watch the game of *boules*, while Thérèse remains at a distance with her back to them. The mother/son relationship is confirmed visually when Mme Raquin wraps Camille in his scarf. When Thérèse and Laurent first meet, the physical space between them is denied by alternating and lingering close-ups registering their immediate emotional affinity. Before the murder, they are relatively free to see each other in the bright, spacious café, but after the crime they are confined to the cell-like dimensions of the lorry's cab, and in uncomfortable proximity. During the judicial enquiry, Thérèse appears as a tiny figure on the steps of the massive court buildings, as though dwarfed by the whole legal process. By contrast, the paralysed Mme Raquin is given a dramatic prominence, now starkly foregrounded in the frame, with the light gleaming in her fixed, accusing eyes. Finally, the collective mindlessness of the board players is suggested by an overhead shot in which they completely fill the frame to assume a single identity.

Carné creates his mood and emphasizes his points by evocative use of sound and lighting. The first appearance of the energetic Laurent is announced by his noisy lorry, while the fateful approach of the blackmailer on his motorcycle is accompanied by ominous musical rhythms. The sentimental theme music swells appropriately, if predictably, to a crescendo as the lovers embrace and, ironically, the happy sounds of a wedding party's romantic waltz drown out Laurent's important telephone conversation with Thérèse. It will be the clock striking five, accompanied by the sound of police sirens, which confirms the fate of the guilty couple. Thérèse's depressed state is expressed through the murky shop, while her happiness is associated with the brighter atmosphere of the café in the park. The fateful train journey is set at night, and the dark station platform together with the eerily-lit train corridors establish a suitable mood of apprehension. When the murder has been committed, the mental turmoil of the protagonists is conveyed by sharp, stabbing shafts of light from a passing train, and the searching police inquiry seems anticipated in the peering headlamp of the speeding locomotive.

A more detailed examination of a selected sequence from the film will serve to illustrate more fully Carné's narrative skills. In the novel, Zola describes how the adulterous lovers are almost surprised by Mme Raquin when she unexpectedly comes up to the bedroom (pp.78-79). The author does not seek to exploit the potential for suspense in his presentation, but in the film, Carné expands this episode to produce a moment of considerable tension.

The sequence is prepared by Thérèse's promise in the park to arrange a more intimate meeting place. A dissolve, with its implied temporal ellipsis, translates the action to the street and the shop. Laurent is seen approaching rather furtively. Thérèse, waiting at the window, observes him taking the side entrance. She opens the door as he climbs the back stairs. Nothing is said, and the couple's silence reinforces the mood of secrecy. These actions are accompanied, however, by a musical score which in turn signals Laurent's apprehensions, and then marks the triumphal achievement of the illicit meeting. The mood is established, and the viewer has been led to identify with the transgressing couple.

A cut to the shop below introduces a second, parallel narrative thread. Mme Raquin is seen to side with a customer complaining about Thérèse, and this confirmation of her ready hostility towards her daughter-in-law brings even greater sympathy for the adulteress. The camera then cuts back to the bedroom corridor to capture Thérèse removing Pompom the cat, who had earlier witnessed the couple's first embraces. The cat's removal implies more intimate moments to come, and the camera, now moving inside the bedroom, shows the couple alone. A smiling Thérèse is relaxed, but Laurent's first words betray his apprehension. Thérèse reassures him that they will not be disturbed.

Once more the camera cuts to the shop, where Mme Raquin, having placated her customer, is horrified to see the cat descending the spiral stairs between the shop and the apartment. The cat has now become the link between the two narrative threads, and in one sense fulfils the fantasy of Zola's characters that he would reveal their adultery. An irritated Mme Raquin, already ill-disposed towards Thérèse, immediately decides to return the cat to her daughter-in-law in the bedroom.

The evident danger for the lovers in this decision is marked by ominous chords as Mme Raquin purposefully climbs the stairs, complaining in rasping tones to Pompom as she does so. Her progress to the bedroom is followed through the apartment, and as her threat to the couple's happiness grows, her movements are accompanied by an ever-more-disquieting musical score. With her knock at the door, the camera cuts to a clearly alarmed Thérèse sitting up in bed, her hair let down, her cardigan removed. Laurent is not to be seen. Mme Raquin flings open the door, and a split-screen effect is produced when a reverse-angle shot, from Thérèse's point of view, frames Mme Raquin in the doorway, with Laurent now revealed behind the open door. Tension evaporates as Mme Raquin withdraws, and her footsteps are heard disappearing down the corridor. After this narrow escape, the couple decide to tell Camille of their affair. Thérèse, hinting that the shock might cause his death, urges Laurent to remain cool. With this decision, the four-and-a-half minute sequence comes to an end.

Carné's alternating, parallel narrative generates suspense. For the most part, the viewer is placed in the privileged position of an omniscient observer as the two economically-presented narrative strands are woven together by using the wandering cat as a structural device. The characters involved in the action have only their limited perceptions: Thérèse and Laurent are blissfully unaware of the approaching threat; Mme Raquin is certainly ignorant of Laurent's presence in the bedroom. Carné has invited identification with the lovers from the outset by establishing them in the sequence before introducing Mme Raquin and her customer. The narrative momentum created by the innocent love scene in the park is thus maintained, and the couple retain the initiative. The viewer, already predisposed to the lovers by the logic of the narrative, is now invited to suspend moral judgement as they meet in the bedroom. Thérèse and Laurent are presented not as transgressors, but as a loving couple under threat from a spiteful Mme Raquin.

The lovers, whom the viewer must assume to be unaware of Mme Raquin's approach, seem vulnerable. Here, Carné has deprived his audience of the omniscience it has so far enjoyed, thus creating tension. Viewers do not know what the camera will disclose when the bedroom door is flung open: they are in the same situation as Mme Raquin. The camera, revealing Thérèse alone on the bed, adopts Mme Raquin's angle of vision, but few in the audience will participate in her aggressive point of view. The reaction-shot of Thérèse in close-up, which records her response to the ominous knock at the door, has already secured the audience's sympathetic identification. When she returns Mme Raquin's piercing gaze, the shot reveals Laurent behind the door, and here the viewer does share not only her angle of vision but her anxious point of view as well. Throughout the sequence, Carné's rhetorical devices, in particular the effects achieved by music and camera-work, distance the audience from the predatory Mme Raquin, while engaging its sympathies on behalf of the lovers.

The relationship which Carné's film enjoys with Zola's novel is seen to be steeped in contradictions. At times, the director's version appears no more than tangential, yet at others to be close in essence, if understandably different in detail and rhetoric. Despite the informed judgements of those critics who see in Carné's film a legitimate cinematic rendering of the author's text, for many readers the screen version will appear to owe no more to Zola's *Thérèse Raquin* than did the author's novel to *La Vénus de Gordes*.

'Imaginez que Furbice ait épousé Margaï...' It was with this proposition that Zola revealed the serialized novel by Adolphe Belot and Ernest Daudet as his inspiration for *Un Mariage d'amour*. Within six months he had turned his short story into *Thérèse Raquin*, though it was to be another six years before a further transformation brought the novel to the theatre. If in the twentieth century other writers have created alternative versions of Zola's fiction, whether for the stage or for the screen, they are continuing in that tradition of adaptation to which the author himself subscribed. Through their transpositions, these writers have paid their own particular homage to Zola's inspired, and inspirational, tale of adultery and murder: *Thérèse Raquin*.

Select Bibliography

EDITIONS

1. *Thérèse Raquin*. Chronologie et introduction par Henri Mitterand, Paris, Garnier-Flammarion, 1970.
2. *Thérèse Raquin*. Edition présentée et annotée par Robert Abirached, Paris, Gallimard, Coll. Folio, 1979.
3. *Thérèse Raquin*. Préface de Henri Guillemin, Paris, Presses Pocket, 1979.
4. *Thérèse Raquin*. Paris, J'ai lu, 1980.
5. *Thérèse Raquin*. Paris, France Loisirs, 1982.
6. *Thérèse Raquin*. Préface de Françoise Xenakis, notes d'Auguste Dezalay, Paris, Livre de Poche, 1984.
7. *Thérèse Raquin*. Paris, EPI, 1984.

ADAPTATIONS

8. Maurette, Marcelle, *Thérèse Raquin, L'Illustration théâtrale*, no. 21 (October 1948), pp.1-31.
9. Rouleau, Raymond, *Thérèse Raquin, l'Avant-Scène Théâtre*, no. 701, (January 1982), pp.3-31.

BOOKS

10. Balázs, Bela, *Theory of the Film*, trans. Edith Bone, New York, Dover, 1970.
11. Best, Janice, *Expérimentation et adaptation. Essai sur la méthode naturaliste d'Emile Zola*, Paris, José Corti, 1986.
12. Bluestone, George, *Novels into Film*, Berkeley, University of California Press, 1957.
13. Carné, Marcel, *La Vie à belles dents*, Paris, Jean-Pierre Olivier, 1975.
14. Carter, Lawson A., *Zola and the Theater*, New Haven, Yale University Press, 1963.
15. Chazal, Robert, *Marcel Carné*, Paris, Seghers, 1965.

16. Goncourt, Edmond and Jules de, *Germinie Lacerteux*, Paris, Nizet, 1968.
17. Hemmings, F.W.J., *Emile Zola*, second edition, Oxford University Press, 1966.
18. Lapp, John C., *Zola before the 'Rougon-Macquart'*, University of Toronto Press, 1964.
19. Perez, Michel, *Les Films de Carné*, Paris, Ramsay, 1986.
20. Zola, Emile, *Correspondance*, éditée sous la direction de B.H. Bakker, 12 vols, Presses de l'Université de Montréal, 1978-.
21. ——, *Œuvres complètes*, édition établie sous la direction de Henri Mitterand, 15 vols, Paris, Cercle du livre précieux, 1966-70.

ARTICLES

22. Boissin, Firmin, 'Romans, contes et nouvelles', *Polybiblion* (1 April 1868), pp.126-27.
23. Claverie, Michel, '*Thérèse Raquin* ou les Atrides dans la boutique du Pont-Neuf', *Les Cahiers naturalistes*, no. 36 (1968), pp.138-47.
24. Doniol-Valcroze, Jacques, 'Le Marin de la Malchance', *Cahiers du Cinéma* , Vol. V, no. 29 (December 1953), pp.41-42.
25. Desonnaz, A., 'Courrier du jour', *Avenir national* (5 December 1867).
26. Dugan, Raymond, 'La psychologie criminelle dans *Thérèse Raquin* et *La Bête humaine* d'Emile Zola', *Travaux de Linguistique et de Littérature*, Vol. XVII, Tome 2 (1979), pp.131-37.
27. Dutourd, Jean, 'Au service de Zola', *Carrefour* (11 November 1953).
28. Furst, Lilian R., 'Zola's *Thérèse Raquin*. A re-evaluation', *Mosaic*, Vol. V, no. 3 (Spring 1972), pp.189-202.
29. Hertz, Henri, 'Emile Zola, témoin de la vérité', *Europe*, Vol. XXX, nos 83-84 (1952), pp.27-34.
30. Jennings, Chantal, '*Thérèse Raquin* ou le péché originel', *Littérature*, no. 23 (October 1976), pp.94-101.
31. Lethbridge, Robert, 'Zola, Manet and *Thérèse Raquin*', *French Studies*, Vol. XXXIV, no. 3 (July 1980), pp.278-99.
32. Mitterand, Henri, '*Thérèse Raquin* au théâtre', *Revue des Sciences humaines* (October-December 1961), pp.489-516.
33. ——, 'Corrélations lexicales et organisation du récit: le vocabulaire du visage dans *Thérèse Raquin*', *La Nouvelle Critique* (November 1968), pp.21-28.
34. Pellerin, H., 'Revue Littéraire. *Thérèse Raquin*, par Emile Zola', *Le Pays* (5 January 1867).
35. Rickert, Blandine, '*Thérèse Raquin*: observations sur la structure dramatique du roman', *Cahiers naturalistes*, no. 55 (1981), pp.42-51.
36. Vigneron, Jean, '*Thérèse Raquin*', *La Croix* (18 October 1981).

37. Vinneuil, François, 'Résurrection de Marcel Carné: *Thérèse Raquin*', *Dimanche Matin* (15 November 1953).

ADDENDUM

38. Schumacher, Claude, *Zola, 'Thérèse Raquin'*, Glasgow, University of Glasgow French and German Publications, 1990.
39. *Thérèse Raquin*, dir. Marcel Carné, Paris, Editions Montparnasse, 1989 (videocassette).
40. Zola, Emile, *Thérèse Raquin*, trans. Pip Broughton, Bath, Absolute Press, 1989.

CRITICAL GUIDES TO FRENCH TEXTS

edited by
Roger Little, Wolfgang van Emden, David Williams

1. **David Bellos.** Balzac: La Cousine Bette.
2. **Rosemarie Jones.** Camus: L'Etranger *and* La Chute.
3. **W.D Redfern.** Queneau: Zazie dans le métro.
4. **R.C. Knight.** Corneille: Horace.
5. **Christopher Todd.** Voltaire: Dictionnaire philosophique.
6. **J.P. Little.** Beckett: En attendant Godot *and* Fin de partie.
7. **Donald Adamson.** Balzac: Illusions perdues.
8. **David Coward.** Duras: Moderato cantabile.
9. **Michael Tilby.** Gide: Les Faux-Monnayeurs.
10. **Vivienne Mylne.** Diderot: La Religieuse.
11. **Elizabeth Fallaize.** Malraux: La Voie Royale.
12. **H.T Barnwell.** Molière: Le Malade imaginaire.
13. **Graham E. Rodmell.** Marivaux: Le Jeu de l'amour et du hasard *and* Les Fausses Confidences.
14. **Keith Wren.** Hugo: Hernani *and* Ruy Blas.
15. **Peter S. Noble.** Beroul's Tristan *and the* Folie de Berne.
16. **Paula Clifford.** Marie de France: Lais.
17. **David Coward.** Marivaux: La Vie de Marianne *and* Le Paysan parvenu.
18. **J.H. Broome.** Molière: L'Ecole des femmes *and* Le Misanthrope.
19. **B.G. Garnham.** Robbe-Grillet: Les Gommes *and* Le Voyeur.
20. **J.P. Short.** Racine: Phèdre.
21. **Robert Niklaus.** Beaumarchais: Le Mariage de Figaro.
22. **Anthony Cheal Pugh.** Simon: Histoire.
23. **Lucie Polak.** Chrétien de Troyes: Cligés.
24. **John Cruickshank.** Pascal: Pensées.
25. **Ceri Crossley.** Musset: Lorenzaccio.
26. **J.W Scott.** Madame de Lafayette: La Princesse de Clèves.
27. **John Holyoake.** Montaigne: Essais.
28. **Peter Jimack.** Rousseau: Emile.
29. **Roger Little.** Rimbaud: Illuminations.

30. **Barbara Wright and David Scott.** Baudelaire: La Fanfarlo *and* Le Spleen de Paris.

31. **Haydn Mason.** Cyrano de Bergerac: L'Autre Monde.

32. **Glyn S. Burgess.** Chrétien de Troyes: Erec et Enide.

33. **S. Beynon John.** Anouilh: L'Alouette *and* Pauvre Bitos.

34. **Robin Buss.** Vigny: Chatterton.

35. **David Williams.** Rousseau: Les Rêveries du promeneur solitaire.

36. **Ronnie Butler.** Zola: La Terre.

37. **John Fox.** Villon: Poems.

38. **C.E.J. Dolamore.** Ionesco: Rhinocéros.

39. **Robert Lethbridge.** Maupassant: Pierre et Jean.

40. **David Curtis.** Descartes: Discours de la Méthode.

41. **Peter Cogman.** Hugo: Les Contemplations.

42. **Rosemary Lloyd.** Mallarmé: Poésies.

43. **M. Adereth.** Aragon: The Resistance Poems.

44. **Keith Wren.** Vigny: Les Destinées.

45. **Kathleen M. Hall and Margaret B. Wells.** Du Bellay: Poems.

46. **Geoffrey Bremner.** Diderot: Jacques le fataliste.

47. **Peter Dunwoodie.** Camus: L'Envers et l'Endroit *and* L'Exil et le Royaume.

48. **Michael Sheringham.** Beckett: Molloy.

49. **J.F. Falvey.** Diderot: Le Neveu de Rameau.

50. **Dennis Fletcher.** Voltaire: Lettres philosophiques.

51. **Philip Robinson.** Bernardin de Saint-Pierre: Paul et Virginie.

52. **Richard Griffiths.** Garnier: Les Juifves.

53. **Paula Clifford.** La Chastelaine de Vergi *and* Jean Renart: Le Lai de l'ombre.

54. **Robin Buss.** Cocteau: Les Enfants terribles.

55. **Tony Hunt.** Chrétien de Troyes: Yvain.

56. **Robert Gibson.** Alain-Fournier: Le Grand Meaulnes.

57. **James J. Supple.** Racine: Bérénice.

58. **Timothy Unwin.** Constant: Adolphe.

59. **David Shaw.** Molière: Les Précieuses ridicules.

60. **Roger Cardinal.** Breton: Nadja.

61. **Geoffrey N. Bromiley.** Thomas's Tristan *and the* Folie Tristan d'Oxford.

62. **R.J. Howells.** Rousseau: Julie ou la Nouvelle Héloïse.

63. **George Evans.** Lesage: Crispin rival de son maître *and* Turcaret.

64. **Paul Reed.** Sartre: La Nausée.

65. **Roger Mclure.** Sarraute: Le Planétarium.

66. **Denis Boak.** Sartre: Les Mots.

67. **Pamela M. Moores.** Vallès: L'Enfant.

68. **Simon Davies.** Laclos: Les Liaisons dangereuses.

69. **Keith Beaumont.** Jarry: Ubu Roi.

70. **G.J. Mallinson.** Molière: L'Avare.

71. **Susan Taylor-Horrex.** Verlaine: Fêtes galantes *and* Romances sans paroles.

72. **Malcolm Cook.** Lesage: Gil Blas.

73. **Sheila Bell.** Sarraute: Portrait d'un inconnu *and* Vous les entendez?

74. **W.D. Howarth.** Corneille: Le Cid.

75. **Peter Jimack.** Diderot: Supplément au Voyage de Bougainville.

76. **Christopher Lloyd.** Maupassant: Bel-Ami.

77. **David H. Walker.** Gide: Les Nourritures terrestres *and* La Symphonie pastorale

78. **Noël Peacock.** Molière: Les Femmes savantes.

79. **Jean H. Duffy.** Butor: La Modification.

80. **J.P. Little.** Genet: Les Nègres.

81. **John Campbell.** Racine: Britannicus.

82. **Malcolm Quainton.** D'Aubigné: Les Tragiques.

83. **Henry Phillips.** Racine: Mithridate.

84. **S. Beynon John.** Saint-Exupéry: Vol de Nuit *and* Terre des hommes.

85. **John Trethewey.** Corneille: L'Illusion comique *and* Le Menteur.

86. **John Dunkley.** Beaumarchais: Le Barbier de Séville.

87. **Valerie Minogue.** Zola: L'Assommoir.

88. **Kathleen Hall.** Rabelais: Pantagruel and Gargantua.